Soul [

CW00539600

Dave,
With all good wishes

Cameron

Being a contemplative in daily life

Cameron Butland

Open Spirituality Publishing

To Chris and Jeff

Open Spirituality Publishing
Copyright 2020 by Cameron Butland
ISBN: 978-0-9926277-2-0

Printed by Book Printing UK
Remus House, Coltsfoot Drive, Peterborough, PE2 9BF

Contents

Foreword by the Rt Rev'd John Stroyan

President of the Association for Promoting Retreats and author of 'Turned by Divine Love'[1]

The longest journey, it has often been said, is from the head to the heart. The western church, unlike her eastern sister, has been and remains deeply marked by this distance. It is this gap between head and heart, between theology and spirituality that '*Soul Desire*' addresses through the medium of contemplative prayer. Theophan the Recluse (1815-1854) identified the essence of true prayer as 'standing before God with the mind in the heart'. A dictum of Orthodoxy is that the theologian is one who prays. In other words whatever we say or write or seek to communicate about God must flow not from intellectual speculation or ideas about God but must flow rather from relationship with God forged in prayer.

When we engage with St Anthony or other desert fathers or mothers what is demanded of us is not so much intellect assent – as in 'I agree with that idea' – but an inward hunger and receptivity to that which speaks to our hearts and can change our lives.

St Symeon the New Theologian (949-1022) identified two forms of apostolic succession within the life of the Church. First, there is the visible apostolic succession of bishops ensuring and guarding the institutional life of the church. Second, and alongside this, is what he calls the 'charismatic' succession of the spiritual fathers and mothers from the apostolic age

---

[1] *Turned by Divine Love* by John Stroyan, BRF, London, 2019

continuing down the generations. It is from this charismatic succession that 'Soul Desire' draws, taking us on a journey, from Anthony to today. The author helps us to encounter and to learn from the holy wisdom of those, throughout the generations, whose lives were rooted in a depth of prayer (where 'deep calls to deep') that attracted and continues to attract to this day, those who are hungry for God.

It has been said that the desert fathers and mothers were not so much teachers as *healers*. Indeed, St Athanasius, his biographer, describes Anthony as 'a *doctor* given by God to Egypt'. Going back further, St Paul recognizes this same distinction between teachers and healers when he writes to the faithful in Corinth: 'Though you have countless guides (*paedagogous* = teachers) in Christ you do not have many fathers. For I became your father in Christ through the Gospel.' 1 Cor.4.15. Paul also uses maternal imagery for this healing or 'whole-making' ministry. To the faithful in Galatia, he writes: 'My little children with whom I am in travail until Christ be formed in you.' Gal.4.19.
One of the notable phenomena in recent years has been the growing number of people seeking spiritual direction. Such people, I venture, are more hungry for wisdom than knowledge and more hungry for healing than teaching. We need, of course, both teaching and healing but there is, I sense, a hunger and a growing hunger for depth, for a meeting with God in our hearts. 'Soul Desire' has much food to offer us here. A particular gift of the book is to (re)introduce us to St Anthony and to use his life and witness as a foundational template for each chapter of the book as we are introduced to different dimensions of contemplative prayer.

Anthony evoked in others what he himself was seeking. The Church, recently institutionalized by the conversion of Constantine, was not enough. Anthony and those who followed him into the desert were hungry for more than the institutional Church could offer. So widespread was this hunger that, as St Athanasius writes, 'the desert became a city'.

Today we see that same hunger for something more, for depth and for a deep connection with God. This is to be celebrated and where '*Soul Desire*' is so timely. Soul desire and the deepest longings and desires of our hearts are a gift of God. Why? Because they come from God. St Anselm prays: 'O Lord give me what you have made me want and grant me what you have made me long for.'

So, this is a timely book responding to a widespread restlessness and need for something more and that 'more' is what God alone can give. It reminds us that contemplation is not reserved for the desert or the monastic life but that it is for all of us, no matter what our context is. It draws us back to the love of God and invites to respond in love. In the words of '*The Cloud of Unknowing*': 'By love he can be grasped but by thought never'.

+John Stroyan
The Bishop of Warwick

Preface

Soul Desire is written for those who are new to contemplation. By its nature this book provides a brief overview of the contemplative tradition. As a result, it is not possible to go into detail about many of the spiritual traditions mentioned. The purpose of the book is to encourage those who seek to be contemplatives in the busy daily lives.

Soul Desire came to be written after a long period of reflection and refinement. This book is rooted in a series of retreats and talks that I have given over the last seven years. Many people are fascinated by the roots of contemplation and the different Christian traditions that have found meaning in apophatic prayer.

In this book, I have established a few simple protocols to simplify the text and to avoid wasteful duplication. As a result, St Antony the Great will simply be referred to as Antony. It is quite correct to spell his name Anthony, but to be consistent throughout I have opted for the shorter form. In addition, I have omitted the St prefix for all saints – the use of this form adds nothing to the text and becomes tedious. Therefore, I will refer to Athanasius not using his full title St Athanasius of Alexandra. For dates, I have used the most commonly agreed date – for example Antony's death in 356 – and have omitted AD after dates as the whole book is dated in the current era. All references are given in footnotes and I will point to sources even when the text paraphrases sayings or stories for the sake of brevity. Hopefully these simple protocols will make the text easier to follow and will not distract the reader.

There are many people I need to thank for their support and encouragement. I am indebted to a number of people for their interest in this subject. Acknowledgment must go to Richard Broughton who directly and indirectly has given me the opportunity to lead a number of retreats on this subject in many different parts of the country. Richard has also kindly edited the style of the text, I am very grateful to him for his advice and time to help getting this book into its final form. In addition, I am grateful to Mark Boyling, who asked me to give a series of talks on this subject at Carlisle Cathedral during Holy Week 2018. Various people have commented on talks I have given and many discussions have taken place on the *Nourishing the Soul* course, which I have helped to lead in Cumbria. I am grateful to a succession of students and colleagues who have helped me to understand some of these issues more clearly than before. I am indebted to Bishop James Newcome for his continued support of my role as spirituality adviser to the diocese and his encouragement for this work.

Special thanks go to those who have shared with me in teaching the various *Nourishing the Soul* courses in Cumbria over the last decade. In particular, I have appreciated the friendship of Chris Wood and Jeff Thomas, to whom this book is dedicated. Chris died during the writing of this book but his influence on my understanding of contemplative prayer has been immense; I will value his memory. Special thanks must also go to Jeff Thomas who has shared my interest in contemplative prayer and generously shared his knowledge, insight, and experience. It is a joy to discuss all of these teachers and their insights with him.
Lastly, I am grateful to my wife Alison for her constant support of my spirituality work.

Cameron Butland, October 2020

Introduction: Contemplative Journey

*A brother asked, 'What good shall I do'? Abba Antony replied,
'Not all works are alike. For scripture says that Abraham was
hospitable and God was with him. Elijah loved solitary prayer,
and God was with him. David was humble, and God was with
him. Therefore, whatever you see your soul desire according to
God, do that thing and you shall keep your heart safe'.*[2]

Antony of Egypt is often regarded as the first contemplative. His
teachings, though, are rooted in the example of Jesus himself.
Antony saw himself as copying the practice of Jesus from the
gospel of St John.

For Antony, there was only one book that told him about Jesus.
Born in the third century, the first half of his life was lived under
extreme persecution of every religion, except that of the
imperial cult. The most extreme of these persecutors was the
emperor Diocletian, 284-305[3], had decreed that all worship of
other gods apart from himself was punishable by death. He even
renumbered the Roman calendar from the date of his birth, so
the years became known as AD, *Anno Diocletian*, in the year of
Diocletian.

Antony, who grew up in the Roman province of Lower Egypt,
saw many of his own family and friends put to death on the
orders of Diocletian for refusing to sacrifice to the emperor. In
his own lifetime Diocletian believed that during his reign of

---

[2] *The Wisdom of the Desert*, Thomas Merton, New Directions,
New York, 1960, p.25.
[3] www.britannica.com List of Roman Emperors

terror he had been successful in suppressing all other faiths. Antony, though, together with his family and friends, continued to keep the Christian faith in secret. The church met despite the great dangers of being discovered or betrayed among the graves, catacombs and neglected places of the city to worship and pray together.

During this early part of his life Antony only knew of the gospel 'kata Johannes' – according to St John. In reading this life of Jesus he knew that prayer was the priority. Jesus drives the traders out of the Temple, rebuking them: 'stop making my Father's house a market-place!'[4] Antony understood first and foremost that for Jesus prayer was the priority, and in following him, Antony needed to make the place of prayer of first importance. In John, the relationship of Jesus to God his Father is the foundation of his relationship in prayer. When he raises Lazarus, Jesus says, 'Father, I thank you for having heard me. I knew that you always hear me, but I have said this for the sake of the crowd standing here, so that they may believe that you sent me'.[5] Prayer is for Jesus a living relationship with God, and Antony understood this from the word 'abide'. He read Jesus saying, 'As the Father has loved me, so I have loved you; abide in my love. If you keep my commandments, you will abide in my love, just as I have kept my Father's commandments and abide in his love. I have said these things to you so that my joy may be in you, and that your joy may be complete'.[6] It is also a

---

[4] John 2:16, *New Revised Standard Version Bible: Anglicized Edition*, copyright 1989, 1995 National Council of the Churches of Christ in the United States of America. Used with permission. All rights reserved worldwide.
[5] John 11:41–42 NRSV, ibid.
[6] John 15:9–11 NRSV, ibid.

relationship of love. This love is threefold between Jesus and his Father, between Jesus and his disciples, and lastly, between the disciples themselves. When Antony was asked to give a 'rule of life' he always refused, rather telling those who questioned him to read the scripture for themselves and to heed the commandment from Jesus to be obedient to love.

Antony is therefore not doing something new in the fourth century when he 'retreats' from the city, following the religious freedom resulting from the Edict of Milan in 313. He sees himself as going back to first principles, placing his life on the first foundations of the example of Jesus. Antony understands Jesus to have prayed silently alone or with his disciples. From John's gospel, he comes to recognise three great principles of this life of prayer: it is the priority of the Christian life, it is rooted in a relationship with God, and that the only purpose in living this prayerful relationship is to be always obedient to love. For Antony, this is the totality of the Christian life.

Antony is clearly practising 'apophatic' prayer. In Christianity, there are two ways of understanding prayer. The cataphatic which means to use our senses, awareness, signs and symbols. In the Western church, we are used to praying in this way. Antony though encouraged praying in silence, the apophatic approach, this is sometimes called 'via negativa', literally meaning 'formless' or 'empty'. Cynthia Bourgeault sees this way of praying as leading us into a deep spiritual relationship, 'we learn that apophatic prayer is far from either formless or empty. It too makes use of faculties but ones that are much more subtle than we're used to and which are normally blocked by overreliance on our more usual mental and affective processing modes'[7]. Apophatic prayer is vital to our understanding of Antony, the advice of the desert teachers and our lives as contemplatives.

Antony is the inspiration of contemplative prayer. His example in the fourth century inspired the 'desert movement' of the next one thousand years. Much of the advice given by these desert fathers and mothers (abbas and ammas) still speaks to us. Much of his teaching was gathered up in *Conferences of John Cassian*[8] and in the five-volume *The Philokalia.*[9] Antony's influence is immense and not to be undervalued. By the time of Antony's death in 356 his influence had extended far beyond North Africa. The quiet deserted places of the ancient world were full of abbas and ammas; Antony's words and wisdom were passed on and added to by succeeding generations of wise teachers. In this century, the contemplative tradition was born and all the great teachers built upon him.

Developing the Contemplative Tradition in the first millennium

Augustine of Hippo was born also in North Africa like Antony in 354. There is no evidence to suggest that Antony ever met the infant Augustine, nor indeed was there a reason or likelihood that the elderly Antony would have had any reason to travel to the place of his birth. Augustine himself was not a

---

[7] *Centering Prayer and Inner Awakening* by Cynthia Bourgeault, Cowley, Lanham, 2004 p.32

[8] *John Cassian Conferences,* Paulist Press, 1985.

[9] *The Philokalia* complete text is available in five volumes translated by G E H Palmer, Faber and Faber, London, 1981–1988. There are several editions of selected writings and extracts available online.

contemplative until much later in life – his first teaching on prayer isn't known until 400, when he would have been forty-six. Augustine also didn't write a rule; rather, he wrote letters and advice in the form of spiritual teaching. His followers, though, created the first 'rule' at the beginning of the fifth century from his writings. The essential teaching of Augustine is the priority of 'silence'. Augustine believed the land itself was 'inhabited with God's silence'. There are many ruined abbeys which were Augustinian in foundation, the most well-known probably being Canterbury Cathedral, like many Norman foundations, it is a continuing Augustinian foundation. The Augustinian tradition of contemplative prayer was championed in England in the eleventh century by the churchmen of the Norman conquest. Martin Laird is the best example of a modern Augustinian, and his book *Into the Silent Land*[10] is its best expression. In many ways though, the centring prayer movement is in the best Augustinian tradition. Thomas Keating[11] and Cynthia Bourgeault[12] represent this teaching in their books.

Benedict of Nursia, who was born in 480 at the beginning of the sixth century, was the first to deliberately write a 'rule',[13] the priority of which is prayer, which supersedes everything else. The rule, though, introduces the idea of three vows made to God but is interpreted and encouraged by the community.

The three vows are obedience – the desire to listen to God and to discern the divine in one another and in the world; stability – not

---

[10] *Into the Silent Land* by Martin Laird, DLT, 2006.

[11] *Intimacy with God* by Thomas Keating, Crossroads, 2009.

[12] Ibid Bourgeault.

[13] *The Rule of Benedict,* translated by Carolinne White, Penguin Classics, London, 2008.

running away' but embracing the person you are, warts and all; and conversion of life – the expectation of change and growth, with discipleship as following where Christ leads. These three vows encourage Benedictines to be very engaged in community development, pastoral care, and championing social justice. Lectio Divina (holy reading) is a practice first developed by Benedict as part of the obedience vow to listen to God in scripture.

Benedict is the first person to give his communities a pattern of prayer to balance times of prayer and practical work. The framework of the times of prayer, though, determines the life of the community. In Benedict's communities, the discipline of the spiritual life first expressed by Antony and Augustine is given a structure.

Benedict died in 543, but his rule doesn't appear to have been followed within the earliest Christian communities in the British Isles. Ninian at Whithorn had made a copy of John Cassian's conferences during his stay with Martin of Tours's community. He brought Martin's example of contemplative prayer to the church as it was expanding its mission in the fifth century. This probably explains why so many of the earliest Christian sites had a high cross dedicated to Martin. Patrick in his 'confession' tells of praying in a contemplative fashion in wild deserted places during his enslavement in Ireland by the U Neills. Following his return to Ireland from Rome in 432, he established Christian communities modelled on Ninian at Whithorn and Martin from Gaul. At this time, it is uncertain if these communities followed any formal rule and it seems unlikely that they would have done.

A century later, though, the British church was mainly founded by religious communities who followed the pattern of Ninian and Patrick but who did have a rule. The rule of Columba, (Columcille in Gaelic) was probably written in the sixth century for his first community at Garton in Donegal, but only fragments still survive. The missionaries of the sixth to eighth centuries prayed according to the teaching of Antony of Egypt and knew of the writings of John Cassian. The rule was practical and rooted in creation. The communities drew their inspiration from the 'little book of revelation' (scripture) and 'the big book of revelation' (creation). Although suppressed by the Norman Augustinian communities of the eleventh century, this spirituality is well represented by many contemporary writers.

There were no vows in this tradition, but rather, a pattern of discipleship. The key principles of what is now called 'Celtic spirituality' are as follows:
- Daily silent contemplative prayer in creation,
- Community prayers at sunrise and sunset,
- Caim (circling) prayer in daily living,
- Central importance of reading scripture and
- Hospitality to the stranger and the offer of the ministry of blessing.

The eleventh century was a time of war, conquest, and violence across Europe. The aggression and violence of the Norman rulers and in the church of Rome afflicted Christian communities across the then-known world, in turn fracturing the unity of the church, splitting in 1054 between East and West and, in Britain, suppressing the vibrant spirituality of Anglo-Saxon Christianity.

Rediscovery of the contemplative tradition in medieval practice

The changes in the church and society in the eleventh and twelfth centuries had a profound impact on the contemplative tradition. In Europe, the fundamental relationship between the praying community and society was fractured.

In England, the new Norman elite suppressed the religious communities, which were the essential fabric of society, not only being the places of vernacular learning, schools, hospitals, social care, and local employment but also places of daily lived contemplative prayerful lives. It is difficult to overestimate the damage done by the Norman Conquest to England. The genocide committed by the new conqueror over the winter of 1068–9 broke the very social fabric of the north. The Anglo-Saxon communities, where local lords lived among their people and the church was part of the Christian communities, were replaced by oppressive Norman lords who didn't speak English and a church where Latin was the language of faith. Rapidly within a generation the religious communities were replaced with parishes and a Norman parish priest, where prayers in English were banned and the people became the passive receivers of the service in Latin. The lively spirituality of the Anglo-Saxons was conquered and oppressed just as much as the land and their livelihoods. At the very edges of the British Isles, this everyday contemplative prayerful tradition was not entirely lost, but for most of Britain and Ireland it was devastated.

In mainland Europe, Francis of Assisi, at the beginning of the thirteenth century, led a rediscovery of contemplation. He lived a radical Christian life which inspired thousands of followers. In many ways his movement was a renewal of the Benedictine way, but he went further and embraced poverty as a virtue. His community valued simplicity and the joy of life. Franciscans, for their origin, have had three orders, the first and second being founded on three vows: poverty, chastity, and obedience. The third order is a lay order and doesn't require these vows, but rather a personal profession of a personal rule. Central to the personal rule is the daily commitment to prayer. There are many stories of Francis which demonstrate his commitment to silent prayer, often following the example of Antony in praying in deserted places. Francis wrote of the 'blessing of tears' in those who came to contemplate afresh and who were often overwhelmed by their first experience of apophatic prayer. His movement spread widely and popularised again contemplative prayer, leading to a rediscovery of the tradition. Modern Franciscans are marked out in their contemplative practice by the same radicalism of Francis himself, best known of whom is Richard Rohr. His Centre for Reconciliation in America, together with his many books and daily podcasts, are very influential in the modern contemplative community. Richard Rohr, though, speaks with a modern voice of Francis, and often his words are challenging and uncomfortable for more conservative believers. But his voice is an authentic expression of the revival led by Francis.

The later medieval church was increasingly attacked from within as the reforms of the eleventh and twelfth century began to unravel. The insistence on the use of Latin rather than vernacular languages led to open rebellion. Many of those who led this rebellion were put to death, such as John Wycliffe, but they encouraged those who followed to rediscover a personal faith. Prayer wasn't to be the exclusive possession of clergy and the church elite. Jan Huss, as a priest himself, recognised this disconnect in Christianity and sought to introduce changes in the fourteenth century. But he was also condemned like Wycliffe and burnt at the stake. Wycliffe and Hus, though, demonstrate that although the church itself was part of a repressive society, there was still a deep longing for a personal practice of silent prayer.

The historian Eamon Duffy[14] has done much in recent years to open our eyes to the realities of the late medieval period prior to Martin Luther's reformation. Many ordinary men and women practised a personal form of prayer very similar to the contemplative tradition from which they had been excluded. Luther's reformation, though, not only released this energy in countries which became known as 'protestant'. The impact of the breakdown in the repression of the late medieval church was felt everywhere.

Ignatius of Loyola was a contemporary of Luther. He was a Spanish soldier who, while recovering from serious injury, developed his 'spiritual exercises' in the sixteenth century. The exercises are demanding and rigorous. His disciples founded the Jesuit order, and as a community, often live in the most extreme and dangerous places. The present pope, Pope Francis, is a Jesuit. The exercises became immediately very popular and it seems that they immediately found a resonance among those who were seeking a more contemplative approach in their daily life.

There are four particular practices. 'The Examen' is a method of prayer that can be used at any time but is usually done at the end of the day. Its fivefold pattern provides a structure for those new to silent prayer and introduces the key elements of Ignatian spirituality. 'Gospel contemplation' is another way of engaging with scripture. It is developed from Lectio Divina but places the

---

[14] *Making the Hours: English and their prayers 1240-1570* by Eamon Duffy, Yale University Press, 2011.

person in their imagination inside the gospel story; it can be a transformative way of using scripture. 'Colloquy' (talking to Jesus) is again in the imagination, where we can place ourselves in the presence of Jesus and listen to what he says to us. Often it is helpful to think of a specific place, such as 'foot of the cross', 'garden of Gethsemane', or 'the upper room'. 'Discernment' is noticing the movement of the Spirit and the images of 'spiritual consolation' and 'spiritual desolation'.

Ignatius, though, is not the only great contemplative teacher of this time. The Carmelite renewal of the sixteenth century also had a remarkable influence in reviving contemplative practice. Although the Carmelites were known from the twelfth century, their distinctive teaching dates from the sixteenth century in the writings Teresa of Avila and John of the Cross. The teaching of these spiritual teachers is that spirituality is about 'longing for God'. Teresa wrote, 'the heart of spirituality is a thirst, a longing for the living God, to know him and to come to a deeper and deeper union with him through prayer even in the here and now'.[15]

This longing can be summarised as 'longing for God in simplicity'. This is marked by giving time each day for solitude and contemplative prayer, decluttering your life, and getting rid of attachments; finding your true centre in God, rather than an 'experience of religion'; 'longing for God in darkness' – John of the Cross uses the image of 'the dark night' to express a growing openness to God during times of illness, poverty, bereavement, old age, and impasse. Spiritual growth comes in the darkness, but 'absence' is painful to bear. Often we need to

---

[15] *Interior Castle* by Teresa of Avila, translated by E Allison Peters, Dover Publications, New York, 2007, p.82.

walk in the darkness in order to find a deep trust in God and 'longing for God through silence'. This is central for Carmelite spirituality. Prayer is not measured by thoughts, words, or emotions, but by simply offering ourselves in God's grace. Prayer is about what God is doing within us rather than anything we can do. Meditation is only the precursor to a prayerful life into which the grace of God fills everything.

Contemplation in the Reformation
The Reformation, though, marked another massive disruption to the contemplative tradition. In England, the sweeping away of the religious communities in the 1530s marked the end of the spiritual powerhouses of silent prayer and contemplation. The religious civil wars under the Tudors, which led to the constant changing of spiritual truth, led to a disconnection from the spiritual life, which was disastrous for society. Eamon Duffy's excellent study *The Voices of Morebath*[16] traces the impact of the religious civil war on one village. The sad and tragic outcome for this small community is emblematic of the impact of the Reformation and the Elizabethan rigorous religious state for ordinary Christians.

The religious tensions couldn't lead to stability and, of course, under the Stuarts, inevitably resulted in the English Civil War, where all the unresolved conflicts of the sixteenth century came to a head. The Restoration in 1660 quickly resulted in an act of religious suppression in 1662 of which Elizabeth I would have been proud. Between 1662 and 1837 religious freedom was suppressed in England, but this resulted ironically in a flourishing of the contemplative tradition in new and unexpected

---

[16] *The Voices of Morebath* by Eamon Duffy, Yale University Press, 2003.

ways. Those who practised these new forms of silent prayer often faced persecution, being thrown out of their homes, jobs and churches, and were forced to the margins of society. Those who would practise their religion in the strictly prescribed manner of the Church of England's prayer book were forced into praying together secretly in houses, barns or even open fields. Yet it was in the lively spirituality of these dissenting groups that contemplative prayer found popular expression.

The Society of Friends
'Be patterns, be examples in all countries, places, islands, nations wherever you come; that your carriage and life may preach among all sorts of people, and to them; then you will come to walk cheerfully over the world, answering that of God in everyone; whereby in them you may be a blessing, and make the witness of God in them to bless you'.[17] These words of George Fox, probably preached in 1656, express powerfully the core belief of the Society of Friends, commonly known as 'The Quakers'. George Fox and the story of Quakerism is rooted in Cumbria. George Fox, though, did not come from Cumbria; rather, he was born in Fenny Drayton, Leicestershire. At the age of twenty-six, he came to a strong personal experience of an inner light. In these years, of course, England was in turmoil as the king fought Parliament. The battles of the English Civil War were the bloodiest ever witnessed on English soil. The brutality and savagery of the killing were typical of civil wars throughout history. This was George Fox's world and explains the absolute focus of Quakerism on pacifism.

---

[17] *The Works of George Fox, Volume Three* by George Fox, Forgotten Books, London, 2015, p.5.

George Fox had a profound religious experience in 1652. Seeking peace and solitude, he climbed Pendle Hill and here had a profound experience of God's presence. As a result, he began to preach in public places and began to draw to himself many of those who were disillusioned with the violent religious division in the English Commonwealth. George's experience in 1652 led him to the unmistakable conclusion that each person should seek a direct, unmediated communion with the Divine, for he stated, 'Christ is come to teach his people himself'.[18]

Despite the peaceful nature of Quakerism, its members suffered greatly in 1662. George Fox and his followers were seen as dangerous radicals set at destabilising the newly restored monarchy. As a result, they were subjected to a systematic persecution depriving many not only of their jobs but also of their liberty. In 1655, George Fox met Margaret Fell. Margaret made her home at Swarthmoor Hall (near Ulverston in the south of Cumbria) a centre for the Society of Friends. The unique nature of Quakerism was not simply in George Fox's rejection of authority and the priesthood, but in recognising the power of silence and contemplation. 'The core of our faith is our living relationship with and the obedience to God, not merely the rote recitation of creeds or performance of rituals'.[19] 'The deeper realities of our faith are beyond precise verbal formulation, and our way of worship based on silent waiting testifies to this'.[20]

---

[18] Ibid., p.122.

[19] 'What do Quakers believe?' by Q. Cadmin, Earlham School of Religion, Quaker Information Centre, 2011, www.quakerinfo.org.

[20] 'Advices and Queries', The Yearly Meeting of the Religious Society of Friends in Britain, 1995, pp. 3–4.

The contemplative revival in Methodism

On 24 May 1738, John Wesley attended a service in Aldgate, London. In this service, he had an experience of his faith being reawakened. 'I felt my heart strangely warmed', he wrote of his experience. 'I felt I did trust in Christ, in Christ alone, for salvation'.[21] His brother, Charles, wrote of the same experience but more poetically, in the words of the hymn 'And can it be':
'My chains fell off, my heart was free,
I rose, went forth, and followed thee'[22]

Wesley's revival was about transformation rooted in contemplation. He spoke of the need for the inner life to change our lifestyle and behaviour. His local societies were much more than a simple meeting place for ordinary working people; they were a place to share experiences of God and the difficulty in walking the way of holiness. The path to holiness was through perfect love, so his message was as much about how to be a Christian as what a believer should believe. Indeed in developing his teaching John Wesley was influenced by reading *The Fifty Spiritual Homilies* by Abba Macarius, and Wesley himself writes of Macarius, that reading him makes 'my heart sing'[23].

In helping those who joined the earliest societies, Wesley offered the idea of a quadrilateral. Jeff Thomas explains this most clearly: 'Wesley believed that the living core of the

---

[21] *What is Methodism*, Cumbria Wesley Historical Society, Carlisle, 2010, p.4.
[22] *Hymns and Psalms*, Methodist Publishing House, London, 1983 (lines from Hymn 216, 'And can it be').
[23] *The First Step toward Grace* by Mark Kurowski, from *Methodist History 36*, January 1998 www.archives.gcah.org

Christian faith was revealed in scripture, illumined by tradition, vivified in personal experience and confirmed by reason. Scripture, however, is primary, revealing the Word of God so far as it is necessary for our salvation'.[24] The class meetings, which were fundamental to the life of his societies, are key to this practical reflection on life, and he often said of the members that they were to 'watch over one another in love'. Wesley's desire was to live a holy life guided by perfect love. In this way, Methodism revived the contemplative tradition rooted in community – in stark contrast to the formal, boring, and stuffy Hanoverian-established church prayer book worship.

Catholic Revival

Following the Catholic emancipation of 1829, there was a considerable revival in contemplative practice across the churches in England. The vicious suppression of Catholic faith (Roman Catholicism as it came to be known after the Reformation) was politically motivated. The usurpation of the monarchy by William and Mary was borne out of a hatred of Roman Catholicism. This led to the celebration of Mass in the open air, in barns or private chapels. This was always a dangerous activity, and there are numerous examples of Roman Catholics being put to death for their faith. This persecution, though, did result in a secret personal piety, a revival of the contemplative tradition as practised by Jesuits and Carmelites. As a result, when Roman Catholicism became legal again in 1829, this sparked a massive upsurge in Catholic prayer and contemplative practice.

---

[24] *Wesleyan Spirituality* by Jeff Thomas (an extract from a talk given to the 'Nourishing the Soul' course on June 18, 2016).

John Henry Newman was the most famous and influential figure of this new Catholic movement in England. Originally, Newman was an Evangelical like Wesley. However, a tour of Italy and a visit to Rome in 1828 changed his views. On hearing John Keble's sermon in 1833 on 'National Apostasy' he became a leader of the newly named Oxford Movement. The Anglo-Catholic renewal, which was to have such an influence upon the Victorian church, was rooted in a personal discipline of prayer and piety. Newman wrote, 'God has created me to do Him some definite service. He has committed some work to me which He has not committed to another. I have my mission. I may never know it in this life, but I shall be told it in the next. I am a link in a chain, a bond of connection between persons. He has not created me for naught. I shall do good; I shall do His work. I shall be an angel of peace, a preacher of truth in my own place, while not intending it if I do but keep His commandments. Therefore, I will trust Him, whatever I am, I can never be thrown away. If I am in sickness, my sickness may serve Him, in perplexity, my perplexity may serve Him. If I am in sorrow, my sorrow may serve Him. He does nothing in vain. He knows what He is about. He may take away my friends. He may throw me among strangers. He may make me feel desolate, make my spirits sink, hide my future from me. Still, He knows what He is about'.[25]

The populist tracts of the movement covered many topics, but advice on prayer was most often the subject. Newman ended his life as a Roman Catholic cardinal, and his influence is across several denominations of the modern church. His vision of the church rooted in sacramental living which has, at its heart, a

---

[25] *John Henry Newman: Spiritual Writings* by John Ford, Orbis, 2012, p.45.

personal relationship within the Trinity in contemplative prayer, has influenced all our churches. The priority of Holy Communion in the main Protestant churches is part of his inescapable legacy.

In the twentieth century, through the work of Evelyn Underhill and Gregory Dix, many came to understand the sacramental significance of personal prayer. Underhill summed this up well: 'Faith is not a refuge from reality. It is a demand that we face reality. The true subject matter of religion is not our own little souls, but the Eternal God and His whole mysterious purpose, and our solemn responsibility to Him'.[26] Her most famous work, *Practical Mysticism*, popularised for a new generation the contemplative tradition and encouraged contemporaries to look to the mystical works of Julian of Norwich and Walter Hilton, signposting a new generation of mystics back to Antony of Egypt.

New Monasticism
The twentieth century, though, of course, was overshadowed by wars in a way unimaginable to previous generations. This frightful legacy of violence, destruction, and death has altered our modern world and society more powerfully than we can often grasp. Yet, as before, this has unleashed a new hunger for contemplative spirituality and led to a distinctive revival.

Dietrich Bonhoeffer wrote, 'The restoration of the church will surely come from a new type of monasticism which has nothing in common with the old but a complete lack of compromise in a life lived in accordance with the Sermon on the Mount in the

---

[26] *Practical Mysticism* by Evelyn Underhill, Stellar Editions, 2014, p.122.

discipleship of Christ'. New Monasticism in the latter half of the twentieth century is a movement that has touched every part of the world and every church, yet it is not one community; rather, it represents a movement which continues to grow and develop.

Bonhoeffer, in laying down the principles for the confessing church in radical opposition to the Nazis, gave a pattern for religious communities around the world. Bonhoeffer coined the phrase 'prayer and righteous action' for New Monasticism. So, all the new monastic communities are marked by his five principles:

- Contemplative prayer,
- Communal living at peace with creation,
- Focus on hospitality,
- Engagement in social justice and
- Working for reconciliation.

In the 1930s, Bonhoeffer met George MacLeod, and he influenced the refounding of the Iona community in 1938 and the subsequent development of Celtic spirituality through communities such as the Corrymeela and Northumbrian groups. Roger Schutz and the community at Taizé were inspired by Bonhoeffer's example, as were 'the base communities' of Latin America. John Wilson and 'The Simple Way' movement used his principles in the 1960s, and this has been further developed by his daughter Ruth in the founding of Rutba House in 2004 in North Carolina. John Main founded the World Community for Christian Meditation (WCCM) as part of this wider movement, although his inspiration came first from eastern spirituality along with Bede Griffiths. Christine Paintner has also developed the 'Abbey Arts Movement' in the last ten years, influenced by this contemplative spirituality.

In many ways, the New Monasticism of the last fifty years brings us closer to Antony, together with the desert abbas and ammas of the fourth century. Increasingly Christian prayer was held in the fragile hands of these local communities of prayer, which may or may not be attached to traditional inherited churches. The vibrancy of these prayer communities embraces the seekers of faith in a way reminiscent of those travelling into the deserts of the fourth century to seek guidance and wisdom.

In this book, I am going to explore this teaching inspired by Antony, the words of the abbas and ammas extolling the 'Prayer of the Heart', discerning the rootedness of contemporary writers in this tradition. Finally, I am going to draw out the consistent teaching of prayer and practice which is applicable to us as modern contemplatives. In this book, as I seek to unlock the contemplative tradition in the teaching of Antony and those who have followed his distinctive way of apophatic prayer, I will offer the reader the principles by which each of us can follow the contemplative path in our daily lives.

Chapter One: Obedient to Love

Jesus said, 'As the Father has loved me, so I have loved you; abide in my love. If you keep my commandments, you will abide in my love, just as I have kept my Father's commandments and abide in his love. I have said these things to you so that my joy may be in you, and that your joy may be complete. 'This is my commandment, that you love one another as I have loved you'.[27]

Antony was born in the third century at the time of persecution. It was a time of martyrdom, and he must have known many who lost their lives. Born during one of many times of persecution, he lived to see the eventual triumph of Christianity under the unification of the empire by Constantine the Great. Despite this new period of religious freedom, Antony sought the same purity of life that he had known growing up in Herakleopolis Magnia (Lower Egypt). Although no longer threatened with physical persecution, Antony came to see the busy life as an equal threat to the inner life of prayer. In renouncing his wealth and career, he took himself into a deserted and lonely place after the example of Jesus to pray to God.

Many others followed him and found Antony in the desert. He didn't seek fame; rather, in his hermit's cell, the inner life explored in contemplative silence. Antony didn't allow anyone to live with him; rather, the men and women who came to him had to build their own cells in the desert. Each seemed to follow his pattern of prayer in the desert. There are many stories of Antony being asked to give a 'rule' of how to live. Antony

---

[27] John 15:9–12.

himself simply referred his seekers to the words of Jesus and his single commandment. For Antony there was only one rule, one pattern, and one commandment, he told everyone to be 'obedient to love'. The words, which we recognise from John's gospel in chapter 15 verses 9–12, were for him at the very heart of his spirituality and contemplative practice of prayer.

There are a number of sources of Antony's life and teaching. It is not possible, though, to write a biography and, indeed, we cannot be certain of the date of his birth. However, within a few years of his death, Athanasius of Alexandria did write a hagiography (which is best understood as a eulogy of a person's holiness). Athanasius's text, although not an easy read for a modern Christian, includes many stories which serve to illustrate Antony's own spirituality.

It is not possible to know when Antony decided to go into retreat from his former life. It would not have been possible to give his life to solitude and prayer prior to 313, as this would have identified him as a Christian and sentenced him to certain death. It seems likely, though, that his decision to lead a solitary life did follow soon after the Edict of Milan. Athanasius says of Antony,

At first he began to abide in places outside: then if he heard of a good man anywhere, like the prudent bee, he went forth and sought him, nor turned back to his own place until he had seen him; and he returned, having got from the good man as it were supplies for his journey in the way of virtue.[28]

---

[28] *Life of St Anthony of Egypt by St Athanasius of Alexandra*, translated by Philip Schaff and Henry Wace, Pantianos Classics, first published 1892, p.6.

Antony, horrified by the hypocrisy of the newfound Christianity of the empire which had formerly so brutally persecuted his family and friends, wanted nothing to do with the Constantine churches. It seems, though, from Athanasius's text that he sought to learn more about the faith from holy men with whose fellowship he had been denied. It would be during this time that he seems to have become aware of other 'scriptures'. He lived at a time before the canons of the Bible had been agreed. Athanasius tells of his diligence, 'He had given such heed to what was read that of the things that were written fell from him to the ground, but he remembered all, and afterwards his memory served him for books.[29] It is important, though, to acknowledge that in his recorded teachings, although Antony does show knowledge of canonical and non-canonical writings, he regarded the gospel of John as having priority. Again and again he returns to the words of Jesus from John's gospel. For him the horror of his persecution as a child and young man seems to have found a sure rock of faith in this gospel.

It seems that shortly after an initial time of talking with and learning from other holy teachers, Antony resolved to live permanently in retreat in the desert. To understand this context better we should remember that the Latin word 'pagan' literally means rural or rustic. In other words, anything outside the city or urban environment was understood as a spiritual wasteland. Antony, in leaving his former life, was in the eyes of his contemporaries going to a wild and dangerous place. Despite the former persecutions, he appears to be deliberately placing his life in danger again. To our modern minds familiar with the concept of 'survivor guilt', this may provide some explanation. To his contemporaries in the fourth century, though, Antony's

---

[29] Ibid., p.7.

vocation was a sign of his faithfulness to God and his discipleship.

Athanasius tells of a strange story of Antony when he had made his decision to leave the city permanently. Once the decision had been made, Antony asked to be locked in the underground tombs outside the place where he was living:

Antony departed to the tombs, and having bid one of his acquaintances to bring him bread at intervals of many days, he entered one of the tombs, and the other having shut the door on him, he remained within alone.[30]

His reasoning and intended purpose in doing this aren't explained, but in many of his sayings Antony contrasts the martyrdom of his youth, including his family and friends being killed in the arena by wild animals, to the 'white martyrdom' of the spiritual battle in the desert. After many days, Athanasius tells of Antony's victory:

And when the enemy could not endure it, but was even fearful that in a short time Antony would fill the desert with the discipline, coming one night with a multitude of demons, he so cut him with stripes that he lay on the ground speechless from the excessive pain. For he affirmed that the torture had been so excessive that no blows inflicted by man could ever have caused him such torment. But by the Providence of God, the next day his acquaintance came bringing him loaves, and having opened the door and seeing him lying on the ground as dead, he lifted him up and carried him to the church. And

---

[30] Ibid., p.10.

many of his kinsfolk sat around Antony as round a corpse. But around midnight he came to himself and arose.[31]

Athanasius suggests that his time in the tombs was not a single event. Rather, he regularly repeated this form of spiritual warfare until whatever it was that drove him into the tombs had passed or been resolved. It is significant that in many of his teachings he speaks of the torture of demons, and the modern reader can only speculate as to what inner demons he had experienced during the traumatic years of persecution. What is clear for us, though, is that he came to see that it was only through self-discipline that he could come to know Jesus in the relationship of love – which he had read in John's gospel – to abide in God, and to know God abiding in him.

Antony's most famous advice – often repeated to all who came to him – that it was enough to sit in your cell attentive to the discipline of prayer seems to be deeply rooted in his earliest experiences. It is the solitary life which demonstrates obedience to the command of Jesus and gives us the fullness of life.

Just as fish die if they remain on dry land so monks remaining away from their cells, or dwelling with men of the world, lose their determination to persevere in solitary prayer. Therefore, just as the fish should go back to the sea, so we must return to our cells, lest remaining outside we forget to watch over ourselves interiorly.[32]

---

[31] Ibid., p.10.
[32] *The Wisdom of the Desert*, Thomas Merton, New Directions, New York, 1960, p.29.

His time with the holy teachers seems to have stayed with him; also, his formative experience in the tombs appears to have taught him the discipline and attentiveness of prayer as his first priority. In his *Texts on Saintly Life,*[33] Antony advocates this 'intelligent' way of life, attacking the hypocrisy of the empire and arguing in favour of the countercultural life he has chosen:

> People are generally called intelligent through a wrong use of this word. The intelligent are not those who have studied the sayings and writings of the wise men of old, but those whose soul is intelligent, who can judge what is good and what is evil; they avoid what is evil and harms the soul and intelligently care for and practice what is good and profits the soul, greatly thanking God. It is these alone who should be properly be called intelligent.[34]

Antony says to those who come to him for advice that it is only their own experience of prayer that can teach them, not his words or the teaching of other holy men. It is this experience of prayer alone that brings us into the divine relationship of love: 'a mind cleaving to God by love, (a God-loving and God-beloved mind) is an invisible blessing, given by God to the worthy for their good life'.[35]

This is our primary relationship that we experience in prayer and through which God leads our lives. It is the obedience to love, through our attentiveness to prayer, that Antony regards as the

---

[33] *Early Fathers from the Philokalia,* translated by E Kadloubovsky and G E H Palmer, Faber and Faber, London, 1954, pp.21–38.
[34] Ibid., p.21.
[35] Ibid., p.28.

true meaning of faithfulness. In *Directions Derived From His Twelve Epistles,*[36] Antony shows that he regards the obedience to love of Christ's command to be the primary route of grace:

God guides all by the action of His grace. Therefore, do not be lazy or lose heart, but call to God day and night to entreat God the Father in his loving-kindness to send you help from above to teach you what to do.[37]

For Antony, though, the soul in relationship with God's love should be skilled in navigating life's inevitable problems and difficulties. Indeed, more than this, though, rooted and grounded in the relationship of divine love should be able to skilfully demonstrate their resilience in times of trouble.

When the wind blows steadily, every sailor can think highly of himself and boast of his skill; but only a sudden change of wind reveals the skill of experienced helmsmen.[38]

For Antony, the commandment to love is the foundation of the relationship with God. Only when the soul seeks God with all its attention, strength, discipline, and commitment can the grace of God be revealed in love. Famously, Antony, who had rejected the Imperial church and its hypocrisy, came to be consulted by the leading bishops at the time of the great councils which have given us the doctrines of Christianity. Antony, though, wanted

---

[36] *Directions of Our Holy Father Antony the Great on Life in Christ, Derived from His Twelve Epistles,* taken from *Early Fathers from the Philokalia,* translated by E Kadloubovsky and G E H Palmer, Faber and Faber, London, 1954, pp.39–55.
[37] Ibid., p.43.
[38] Ibid., p.43.

nothing to do with such debates and meetings; his priority was the solitary life of prayer. On one occasion, a group of bishops came to ask his advice on the nature of Christ. How could Jesus be truly human and divine? Antony received them with hospitality but wouldn't discuss the topic of Christology; rather, he fussed around his cell tiding and doing minor jobs. Eventually the eminent bishops insisted that he should give them his answer. Antony then agreed but only he had one final task to do, for which he asked their help. The day was ending and dusk was falling; he needed urgently to get his chickens into the safety of their coup. For some time Antony and the bishops chased the chickens around the yard before finally locking them up safely – sore, scratched, and out of breath, Antony sat down the bishops to deliver his answer.

'Do you understand what I have shown you?' he asked, the bishops looked bemused, he hadn't shown them anything. 'What did you learn from the chickens?' he asked, they became annoyed, they were bishops of the church, they didn't come to be insulted by this old hermit. 'Learn the lesson of your experience', Antony told them, 'and you will find the answer to your question'.

Then he gently explained to them that he had no way to explain to his chickens each night why they must return to their coup. After all, they had no knowledge of the dangers that surrounded them: the wild beasts, the robbers, the cold, and other dangers. Each evening they squawked and scratched him. If only he could become a chicken for one day he could explain in a way they would understand and show them how to find safety for themselves. Learn the lesson, he told them, for this is exactly what God had done in Jesus. He had entered into the world, lived a human life, both fully human and divine to show us the way to live in safety and in peace.

This story tells us many things about Antony. His sense of humour, delighting in taking down the pompous bishops and giving them a lesson in humility. At the same time, it demonstrates his gentle teaching taking examples from the natural world to illustrate and explain. Most of all it speaks of his fundamental relationship with the divine, his understanding of the experience of being obedient to love, his knowledge of the divine love abiding in him, and how in relationship with God he could know his goodness and grace.

By the time of Antony's death in 356, the desert was full of holy men and women, known as abbas and ammas (meaning fathers and mothers). Antony became the first 'religious' and from his example the traditions of the religious life begin. Antony, though, is also the first to practise the form of silent prayer that became the contemplative life that was written about by John Cassian in the Western church and the foundation of the eastern prayer of the heart. His distinctive pattern and teaching of prayer came to be known as contemplative prayer, and in the next chapter we come to learn more of this loving form of personal prayer.

Chapter Two: Loving Prayer

When it was evening on that day, the first day of the week, and the doors of the house where the disciples had met were locked for fear of the Jews, Jesus came and stood among them and said, 'Peace be with you'. After he said this, he showed them his hands and his side. Then the disciples rejoiced when they saw the Lord. Jesus said to them again, 'Peace be with you. As the Father has sent me, so I send you'. When he had said this, he breathed on them and said to them, 'Receive the Holy Spirit'.[39]

The desert fathers and mothers taught those who came to them about the 'prayer of the heart'. This is the inner life of which we become aware through silent prayer. The silence of the Spirit allows us to know the unconditional love of God. This leads us to live humbly before God. The prayer is therefore not about words, but rather emptying ourselves before our creator – 'apophatic prayer'. God truly knows us better than ourselves. God also loves us better than we can, for God has already accepted us as we are – something we find almost impossible to believe. Antony told those who came to him to be obedient to love. How can we do that, though? Only by opening our hearts and by recognising all we need is already given to us in love can we be obedient to love. Once we know the unconditional love which holds and guides us, then we can we show forth that love in all we say and do – most of all in our loving prayer.

In the Eastern Church, the prayer of the heart is a significant spiritual resource. In the West, we have lost sight of much of

---

[39] John 20:19–22.

Antony's teaching and all that flowed from it. Only in recent years have we begun again to hear this ancient teaching. *The Philokalia* is a collection of the sayings of Antony together with many of the writings of the desert fathers and mothers which speak of the loving prayer, which is the response of the prayer of the heart. In seeking this wisdom, we are drawn closer again to the nature of God and the love which is deep within us.

Antony's distinctive way of praying was noted by his contemporaries, and those who sought his advice prompted some of his most famous teaching. One monk came to Antony at the end of his life and asked the holy man why he couldn't pray as he did. Antony replied that learning to pray was like learning to swim in the sea. When you first approach the sea, the new swimmer is apprehensive, and so, first of all, the person will stand at the water's edge. The new swimmer will feel the water, how warm or cold it is and what it feels like on their skin. The person can see the horizon and where they have come from on the shore. Antony said that coming to silent prayer is the same. It is unfamiliar and it takes some time to observe the chatter of the mind whilst still being aware of the world and its distractions.

Next, Antony said that as the swimmer becomes confident in the sea, the person moves further into the water but keeps their feet on the ground. The person can still see the horizon and where they have come from on the shore. Again, Antony said this is like the movement into contemplative prayer. The seeker comes to understand that this form of prayer is different. Yet they still haven't experienced contemplation, for they are distracted by the world around them.

The next stage is when the swimmer begins to swim in the sea. They are unconfident and also have to return to the shore for reassurance. The swimmer doesn't give himself completely to the water, and so their head is still above the water. The person can still see the horizon and where they have come from on the shore. In a similar way, as the person enters into the practice of silent prayer, they are aware of the technique of praying and often have to return again to their verse to be attentive to the silence and quietening the mind. But they are still distracted.

Finally, said Antony, though there comes a moment when as with the swimmer in the sea, the person comes to trust the water and is held by it. The water is all around the swimmer; they are only aware of the way they are held and the water surrounding them. No longer can the person can see the horizon and where they have come from on the shore. This is the way of contemplative prayer. There comes a time when the person is no longer distracted or thinking of their technique, rather they are immersed in the love of God and live in the moment entirely in his love.[40]

Antony's advice to those who sought guidance about how to pray was often very simple and clear. He used many everyday images to teach. Antony used images of house building, sailing boats, shopping in markets, birds in flight, and creation. Indeed, Antony understood that everything in creation was God's classroom, replying to a distinguished visitor in this famous exchange:

A certain philosopher asked Antony, 'Father, how can you be happy when you are deprived of the consultation of books?

---

[40] *Writings from the Philokalia on Prayer of the Heart,* translated by E Kadloubovsky and G E H Palmer, Faber and Faber, London, 1951, pp.130–131.

Antony replied, 'My book, O philosopher, is the nature of created things, and any time I want to read the words of God, the book is before me'.[41]

Antony's often repeated advice to those who had abandoned contemplative prayer – finding it too difficult and giving up – was to begin by asking a simple question: what happens every day in the east? The troubled enquirer might look confused but eventually stumble to the reply, 'Every day? The sun rises!' 'Yes', Antony would reply, 'every day is a new day, and every day we can begin again to pray and resolve again to be disciplined in the prayer of the heart'.

For Antony, everything was rooted and grounded in prayer. There are many examples of his encouragement of others.
Certain of the brethren said to Antony, 'We would like you to tell us some word, by which we may be saved'. Then Antony said, 'You have heard the scriptures, they ought to be enough for you'. But they said, 'We want to hear something also from you, Father'. Antony answered them, 'You have heard the Lord say, If a man strikes you on the left cheek, show him also the other one'. They said to him, 'This we cannot do'. Antony said to them, 'If you can't turn the other cheek, at least take it patiently on one of them'. They replied, 'We can't do that either'. Antony said, 'If you cannot do that, at least do not go striking others more than you want them to strike you'. They said, 'We cannot do this either'. Antony said to another disciple, 'Go cook some food for these brethren, for they are very weak'. Finally, Antony said to them, 'If you cannot even do this, how can I help you? All I can do is pray'.[42] Antony here is operating as the wise holy

_____

[41] Merton op. cit. p.62.
[42] Ibid., p.76.

man trying to encourage this group, but he reminds them in the end all that we can do is to hold each other in prayer.

The lesson of holding each other in prayer is one that Antony had to learn himself during the earliest days of his retreat. Having spent his time in the tombs, he then went and lived in a ruined fort before travelling further away from towns and villages towards the coast. Here in a deserted place he built his cell, not allowing anyone who sought his advice to settle nearby but rather to leave once he had answered their questions. Antony, in describing this time in his solitary life, was brusque, even rude to his enquirers. He couldn't understand why they were being sent to him by the Holy Spirit, and was often irritated by these interruptions which he felt were distractions to the inner life of prayer, the 'white martyrdom' of his disciplined life of contemplation. Yet Athanasius says that he was unsettled in this time, perhaps for up to twenty years. He felt he had dedicated his life to God but was still unfulfilled. Antony prayed that he might be shown the way, that God might reveal to him what he was missing in his contemplative life. He had disciplined himself in the life of prayer and yet he didn't feel that it was enough.

Over time, Antony came to get the sense that he should again seek out holy men and women who might show him where he was falling short. He began to walk from village to village, town to town, seeking out holy teachers. As he prayed, he discerned that the Spirit would lead him to one who was living a more holy life then he was following. Eventually he came to a town on the edge of the desert, and he heard of a holy man who lived there. Everyone spoke of this saintly person who gave them great encouragement and taught all who came to him. Antony went to the town centre and was told the holy man was in the market. Again, he asked where he was, and then found out that the holy man was the town's cobbler and was sitting outside his shop. Antony approached him as was warmly welcomed, the holy man invited him to stay with him and his family.

Antony was unimpressed. After he had given up his home and lived in the desert, this man lived amid the distractions of the town. How could he be holier? Antony had renounced the attachments of living with other people to be solely attentive to prayer; how could this man give himself to contemplation surrounded by his noisy family? How could he be more prayerful? Antony had given away all his money to live a simple life dependent upon God's goodness; this man traded in the market. How could he be more worthy in wealth than Antony was in poverty? Antony challenged him, and the holy man answered that he was right. He was distracted by the town, the demands of his family, and that he could only give one third of everything he received to the poor. When he prayed, he told Antony, he couldn't spend all day praying in a cell, but what he could do was silently pray for everyone who passed by in the market, and in this was holding each person in prayer after the teaching of the Lord in the gospel, being obedient to love in his prayer. Antony realised why he had been brought to meet this holy man and how he needed to change. Antony recognised the discipline of the contemplative was not solely about his inner journey but was for the purpose of holding others in loving prayer.

What this story of Antony should show us is the foundation of the contemplative tradition. Often, we think of prayer as something we say or do. This is not the meaning of prayer for Jesus, and this is what Antony discerned. Jesus gives us an example of prayer as a relationship: a relationship with God and us. 'Abide in me as I abide in you', Jesus tells his disciples. This relationship means that the whole of our life is to be lived prayerfully. There is nothing separate from the Creator and the Spirit in our discipleship. How we pray is therefore as important as what we pray. This is where the example of Antony speaks to the modern contemplative. Antony was a man rooted and grounded in prayer, but hadn't until this time discerned both the inwards and outwards movement of the Spirit. Antony believed that St John's gospel was the most important book in scripture and read there the commandment of Jesus 'to love one another as I have loved you'. Antony knew that prayer is a relationship of love. In silent prayer Antony came to the knowledge of this truth very simply – that 'silence is the language of the Spirit'.

Many of the issues Antony's world faced are the same as ours: threats of war and violence, pandemics and plagues, climate catastrophe and economic collapse. People asked what we can do in our world when we feel so powerless to make a difference. Apologetically, we sometimes mumble that we could say 'a prayer, if you like'. We should be much more positive than this half-hearted response. Our calling is to put prayer first, as revealed to Antony. When facing any new situation, sudden illness, grieving, or overwhelmed by the world's suffering – our first response, always and everywhere, should be prayer. As the Orthodox Christians call it, 'the Prayer of the Heart'. A silent trusting relationship rooted in love, which is contemplative prayer. Antony believed all was in God's hands, he believed that God knew all needs before they were asked, and he believed that everything is Spirit-filled. Antony didn't need to say anything else, rather, to focus his attention in prayer on those who were facing great danger. Antony has provided the example of holding on in love together, uniting prayers not for the sake of the churches, but rather for those around us and those facing enormous pressures.

Like many other people, I have seen the power of prayer to change and transform lives, but that power comes not from us; rather, it comes from the Spirit working through the world. Like Antony we are called to witness to this truth by trusting in loving prayer that God is faithful and good. Antony's sister, Theodora, came to understand also the fundamental nature of contemplative prayer:

> A teacher ought to be a stranger to the desire for domination, vainglory and pride. A teacher should not be fooled by flattery, nor blinded by gifts, conquered by the stomach, nor dominated by anger. A teacher should be patient, gentle and humble as far as possible; successfully tested and without partisanship, full of concern and a lover of souls.[43]

Theodora here expresses what Antony came to recognise in the discipline of silent prayer: that in knowing that God was within, illuminating his life. In the same way, God was within each human life, and with this was the potential to bring light into every life. He was reminded of the familiar words from John's gospel: 'what has come into being in him was life, and the life was the light of all people . . . the true light which enlightens everyone'. [44] Antony came to understand that in the contemplative life, which he had dedicated himself to, he needed to become, in the words of his sister, 'a lover of souls'.

The object of 'the prayer of the heart' is, in the words of Thomas Merton, to find our true resting place. This is what had been revealed to Antony. Merton, in his study of a collection of

---

[43] *The Desert Mothers* by Mary Earle, Morehouse Publishing, 2007, p.39.
[44] John 1:4, 9.

Antony's sayings along with other early desert fathers and mothers of the fourth century called the *Verba Seniorum*, comments:

> The proximate end of all this striving was purity of heart, a clear unobstructed vision of the true state of affairs, an intuitive grasp of one's own inner reality as anchored in God through Christ. The fruit of this was quies, rest. The rest which they sought was simply the sanity and pose of a being that no longer has to look at itself because it is carried away by the freedom that it is in. And carried where? Wherever love itself, or the divine spirit, sees fit to go. Quies, then, was a kind of simple nowhereness and nomindedness that had lost all preoccupation with a false or limited self. Antony remarked that 'the prayer of the monk is not perfect until he no longer realizes himself or the fact that he is praying'.[45]

Antony shows us that love is the spiritual life. The primacy of loving prayer is above all. For Antony and the desert fathers and mothers, loving prayer takes precedence over everything: knowledge, discipline, scripture, solitude, the church. It is the primary relationship with the divine. Merton understands this radical inspiration in Antony's when he says:

> Love demands complete inner transformation, for without love we cannot come to identify ourselves with another. We have to become, in some sense, the person we love. And this involves a kind of death of our own being, our own self.[46]

---

[45] Merton op. cit. pp.8–9.
[46] Ibid., p.19.

We need to understand what this life of loving prayer means for Antony. We need to understand this way as he has demonstrated it for all who follow him. The primacy of loving prayer for Christians is what our faith has to offer our world; when we see 'the faith' as being simply the church, we miss this greater truth. As each generation has rediscovered and valued the teaching of Antony and prayerful experience of the desert, we can come to know afresh that our only priority is loving prayer and everything is of lesser importance. This is our calling, this is our discipleship and this is our journey.

Chapter Three: Loving Community

Jesus prayed, 'Sanctify them in the truth; your word is truth. As you have sent me into the world, so I have sent them into the world. And for their sakes I sanctify myself, so that they also may be sanctified in truth. I ask not only on behalf of these, but also on behalf of those who will believe in me through their word, that they may all be one. As you, Father, are in me and I am in you, may they also be in us, so that the world may believe that you have sent me. The glory that you have given me I have given them, so that they may be one, as we are one, I in them and you in me, that they may become completely one, so that the world may know that you have sent me and have loved them even as you have loved me. Father, I desire that those also, whom you have given me, may be with me where I am, to see my glory, which you have given me because you loved me before the foundation of the world'.[47]

Antony didn't establish an organisation. Rather, Antony sought the solitary life. In seeking this, he did not renounce community; rather, he recognised the need for his own space in the first place to come to know the divine love within. However, in seeking silence, Antony found, as millions have done ever since, that silence is deeply attractive to others. In seeking to be alone, he found community.

The paradox of finding community in solitude is reflected upon by John Main: 'In meditation we develop our capacity to turn our whole being toward the Other. We learn to let our neighbour be, just as we learn to let God be. We learn not to manipulate

---

[47] John 17:17–24.

our neighbour but rather to reverence them, to reverence their importance, the wonder of their being; in other words, we learn to love. Because of this, prayer is the great school of community'.[48]

In the tenth of John Cassian's conferences, Abba Issac, living at the end of the fourth century, spoke of the unity in community of those who followed the path of silent prayer:

> So it shall be, when our every love, desire, eagerness, effort and thought, all that we live, speak, breathe, will be God. And that unity which is now the Father's with the Son and the Son's with the Father will have transfused our perception and mind, that is, so that just as with a sincere and pure and indissoluble love He loves us, we too will be joined to Him by perpetual and inseparable delight, so linked to Him, to be sure, that whatever we breathe, understand, say, would be God. In Him, I say, we shall accomplish the end about which we spoke earlier, the which the Lord besought that it would be fulfilled in us when He prayed, "That they all may be one just as We are one, I in them and You in Me, that they too may be perfected in one", and again "Father, I wish that those whom You have given Me may themselves be with Me where I am".[49]

Abba Issac's words represent Antony's teaching. Antony speaks of the 'goal of perfection'; the purpose of the contemplative life is to develop 'sacred unity'. By turning inwards in

---

[48] *Word into Silence: A Manual for Christian Meditation* by John Main, Canterbury, 2006, p.78.
[49] *Saint John Cassian on Prayer,* translated by A M Casiday, SLG Press, Oxford, 2006, pp.41–2.

contemplative prayer, John Main reminds us this turns us outwards as well. The understanding of the earliest desert fathers is that the solitary's destination is the goal of being worthy of blessedness; as Abba Issac says, 'The end of all perfection, so that every day the mind, may be lifted towards spiritual things, until its whole life and the heart's every thought are made on continuous prayer'.[50]

John Main again reminds us that the goal of perfection, which might seem individualistic, actually turns us outwards in fellowship as Christ's body.

> In prayer, we realize the true glory of Christian community as a fellowship of the anointed, living together in profound and loving mutual respect. Christian community is in essence the experience of being held in reverence by others and we in our turn reverence them. This reverence for each other reveals the members of the community as being sensitively attuned one to the other on the wavelength of the Spirit, the same Spirit that has called each of us to fullness of love. In others, I recognize the same Spirit that lives in my heart, the Spirit that constitutes my real self. Even if our ideas or principles clash, we are held in unison, by our mutual recognition of each other's infinite lovableness, importance and essential unique reality.[51]

The contemplative path of Antony continued to attract others throughout his life in the desert, so much so that Athanasius commented, 'While Antony was speaking all rejoiced; in some the love of virtue increased; in others carelessness was thrown

---

[50] Ibid., p.42.
[51] Main op. cit. p.79.

aside; the self-conceit of others was stopped; and all marvelled at the grace given to Antony from the Lord for discerning of spirits'.[52] In a famous passage, he gives a vivid picture of the vitality and vibrancy of the lives of the earliest desert fathers and mothers inspired by the example and teaching of Antony:

> So their cells were in the mountains, filled with holy bands who sang psalms, loved reading, fasted, prayed, rejoiced in the hope of things to come, laboured in almsgiving, and preserved love and harmony one with another. And truly it was possible, as it were, to behold a land set by itself, filled with piety and justice.[53]

Mary Earle, in her book on the example of the desert mothers, speaks of this example of community life:

> In the fourth century the desert of Egypt was full of men and women seeking to live out the 'Great Commandment'.[54] There were also pilgrims and seekers going to the ammas and abbas to seek counsel, to ask 'Give me a word'.[55]

The contemplative movement begins within this rapid development, which is both individual and corporate. Many of the sayings from the *Verba Seniorum* are imbued with this underlying movement, which is at the same time the Spirit filled inwards to outwards dynamic. The story of Abba Anastasius and his stolen book provides a perfect example.

---

[52] Athanasius op. cit. p.26.

[53] Ibid. p.26.

[54] 'In everything do to others as you would have them do to you', Matthew 7:12.

[55] Earle op. cit. p.73.

A story is told of Abba Anastasius, who wrote a fine book full of devout teachings, beautifully crafted, which was 'worth at least a year's wages'. One day, a certain monk came to see Anastasius, and as night fell, he departed secretly, stealing the book for himself. The next day, when Anastasius came to read from the book, he could not find it and realised that it must have been stolen the previous day by his visitor. He, though, did not send a message to ask for his book to be returned for fear that the sin of perjury might be added to the sin of theft. In the meantime, the monk took Anastasius's book to a local market to sell it. In the market, the dealer was impressed by the book and told the monk to return the next day, when he would give him what it was worth. The dealer then took the book to Abba Anastasius as he knew him to be a wise and holy man who would know the book's value. When he saw the book, Anastasius immediately recognised it but didn't tell the dealer that it belonged to him; rather, he said it was 'worth at least a year's wages'. The following day, the monk returned, and the dealer told him that he had had the book appraised by Abba Anastasius and that it was 'worth at least a year's wages'. The monk asked the dealer, 'Is that all he said? Did he not make any other remarks?' 'No', replied the dealer. Upon hearing this, the monk refused to sell the book and ran to Abba Anastasius, taking the book and weeping loudly. Anastasius, though, wouldn't accept the book, saying, 'Go in peace, brother. I make you a present of it'. But the monk replied, 'If you do not take it back I shall never have any peace'. Thereafter, the monk spent the rest of his life as a companion of Abba Anastasius.[56]

This story of Abba Anastasius is typical of the desert community. The goodness of the holy teaching bringing the

---

[56] Story paraphrased from Merton op. cit. pp.30–31.

disciple to humility and love to their senses. A mutual dependence of generosity and compassion enacting the loving community of the contemplatives seeking to become the body of Christ. Abba Pastor is quoted in the *Verba Seniorum* encouraging others to live out the life of loving prayer in the loving vocation of the community:

> If you have a chest full of clothing, and leave it for a long time, the clothing will rot inside it. It is the same with the thoughts in our hearts. If we do not carry them out by physical action, after a long while they spoil and turn bad.[57]

Antony may not have given a 'rule of life' and physically lived close by to others, but his pattern of prayer encouraged others to live in a way which was open and compassionate, without judgment of others' motives. This is an example of recognising and discerning the divine within each other.

Theoleptus writes in *The Philokalia* nearly a thousand years after Antony extolled his pattern of life:

> Monkhood is a tall and fruitful tree, the root of which is renunciation of everything worldly; its branches, the absence of all attachments in the soul; its fruit, the wealth of virtues and love inspired by God and the joy in others which is inseparable.[58]

---

[57] Merton op. cit. p.42.

[58] *Writings from the Philokalia on Prayer of the Heart,* translated by E Kadloubovsky and G E H Palmer, Faber and Faber, London, 1951 p.383.

Theoleptus, as the Metropolitan of Philadelphia in Greece, encouraged those who wished to become fully Christ's disciples to embrace the contemplative life. For in the practice of silent prayer, he said, true harmony of mind, word and soul were to be found. After the example of Antony, this harmony in the individual in turn brings unity in divine love to all who follow in this way together.[59]

Rowan Williams notices this aspect of the contemplative life when he commented:

> One thing that comes very clearly from any reading of the great monastic writers of the fourth and fifth centuries is the impossibility of thinking about contemplation or meditation of "spiritual life" in abstraction from the actual business of living in the Body of Christ, living in concrete community. The life of intimacy with God in contemplation is both the fruit and the course of a renewed style of living together.[60]

In this reflection on the desert fathers and mothers by Rowan Williams is the sense of a loving community; individuals, through turning inwards in contemplation, are then turned out by the experience of divine love. It is this community of divine love which is the fulfilment of the prayer of Jesus himself, 'that they may be one, as we are one, I in them and you in me, that they may become completely one'.

Contemplative prayer therefore leads us to recognise the divine in one another. It is a vocation to silence, and in silence we can

---

[59] Ibid., p.390 (article 19).
[60] *Silence and Honey Cakes* by Rowan Williams, Lion, 2004, p.22.

come to know the language of the Holy Spirit. In coming so completely into the heart and soul of our inner life, we come to understand more clearly the true life of Jesus, which is our pattern and example every bit as much as it was for Antony and those desert teachers. The community of contemplatives within the Christian faith isn't always easy to spot or to recognise, yet wherever the faith is to be found among the poorest and most in need, often it is lived out by a community of contemplatives.

In the last one hundred years, the practice of contemplative prayer has been found in many forms of new monastic style communities from Iona to Taize, from the Confessing Church to Latin American–based communities, from Corrymeela to 'The Simple Way'; these houses of prayer have turned inwards to move outwards. The example of Antony lives on in these communal houses of contemplation.

The way of silence is therefore the way of community.
However, Antony gave his community no rule (this gradually emerged in the centuries that followed – most famously Benedict's rule became the measure of the religious life many centuries later). Many Christians who followed Antony's practice like him have resisted the call to found an institution. Rather, they, like Antony, called men and women to respect the divine within each human heart and to seek God themselves rather than judging others. As we seek silence, we will inevitably be drawn closer together in love and will need to explore together what community means for us.

Thomas Merton sums up these loving communities, which still challenge our modern Christianity:

> The flight of these contemplatives into the desert was neither purely negative nor purely individualistic. They were not

rebels against society. True, they were in a certain sense "anarchists" and it will do no harm to think of them in that light. They did not believe in letting themselves be passively guided and ruled by a decadent state. They believed that there was a way of getting along without slavish dependence on accepted, conventional values. But they did not intend to place themselves above society. They did not reject society with proud contempt, as if they were superior to others. On the contrary, one of the reasons why they fled from the world was that in it people were divided between those who were successful and imposed their will on others, and those who had to give in and be imposed upon. The desert fathers and mothers declined to be ruled, but at the same time had no desire to rule over others. Nor did they fly from human fellowship, the very fact that they are still known to us is that they uttered these words of advice to one another is proof that they were eminently social. The society they sought was one were all were truly equal, where the only authority under God was the charismatic authority of wisdom, experience and love.[61]

---

[61] Merton op. cit. pp.4–5.

Chapter Four: Loving Heart

When Mary came where Jesus was and saw him, she knelt at his feet and said to him, 'Lord, if you had been here, my brother would not have died'. When Jesus saw her weeping, and the Jews who came with her also weeping, he was greatly disturbed in spirit and deeply moved. He said, 'Where have you laid him?' They said to him, 'Lord, come and see'. Jesus began to weep. So the Jews said, 'See how he loved him!'[62]

Antony, in telling his followers to be obedient to love, was not giving them a rule. Rather, Antony was trying to remind them of Jesus and the pattern of his life. For those who followed Antony's pattern of silent prayer, the example of Jesus was paramount. They saw Jesus as the perfect model of the faithful life and the loving nature of God. It is the loving heart of Jesus himself supremely as shown in John's gospel that the desert fathers and mothers call on all to follow. Writing at the beginning of the fifth century, Hesychios encourages his disciple Theodoulos to emulate Christ:

> Just as a man blind from birth does not see the sun's light, so one who fails to pursue watchfulness does not see the rich radiance of divine grace. Attentiveness is the heart's stillness, unbroken by any thought. In this stillness, the heart breathes and invokes, endlessly and without ceasing, only Jesus Christ who is the Son of God and Himself God.[63]

---

[62] John 11:32–37.

[63] *The Philokalia Volume 1,* translated by G E H Palmer, Philip Sherrard, and Kallistos Ware, Faber and Faber, London, 1979, p.163.

For the contemplative, therefore, this life is not about merely copying Christ but rather coming to recognise the loving heart, to discern in stillness that heart within. The key quality is humility in following Jesus. Hesychios tells Theodoulos, 'Let us learn humility from Christ'.[64] Again, he says, 'Let your soul trust in Christ'[65] and then finally, 'Watchfulness is a graceful and radiant virtue when guided by Christ'.[66] The words of Hesychios are drawn from a deep well of teaching among the desert tradition; humility is a key quality which marks out the contemplative way as very different from the Imperial Church of the fourth century. What Merton describes as a form of anarchic behaviour is perhaps better understood as a radical desire to be in Christ; humility demonstrates that they are in Christ and he is in them.

Merton understands that Antony demonstrates in his life and teaching the qualities of Christ's loving heart. 'The basic realities of the interior life are there', he comments, 'faith, humility, clarity, meekness, discretion and self-denial'.[67] To these, Merton himself adds 'common sense', and by this, he means a down-to-earth quality in the lives of the desert fathers and mothers that is immediately attractive and recognisable from the gospel. Quoting the example of several early abbas who demonstrated their loving heart in deeds as well as words, he comments:

---

[64] Ibid., p.169.
[65] Ibid., p.170.
[66] Ibid., p.171.
[67] Merton op. cit. p.13.

We read of Abba Ammonas who spent fourteen years praying to overcome anger, or rather more significantly, to be delivered from it. We read of Abba Serapion, who sold his last book, a copy of the gospels, and gave the money to the poor, thus selling the very words which told him to sell all and give to the poor. Another abba severely rebuked some monks who caused a group of robbers to be thrown in jail, and as a result the shamefaced hermits broke into the jail by night to release the prisoners.[68]

Humility is not a quality which is an aspiration or a technique to be employed; rather, it is the expression of the faithful contemplative being rooted in the loving heart of Jesus. Abba Barsanuphius sees humility as being the true home of the contemplative: 'Internal work is a headache that brings forth purity, and purity generates a lull of the heart that brings forth humility. By humility man becomes a dwelling place for the Lord'.[69] Often the desert fathers and mothers, though, also show their humour and therefore their humanity in the advice they give. 'Without humility some angels became devils, and with humility some devilish people became angels', comments Abba John el-Daragi. It is a gentle humour which serves to both make their teaching memorable as well as challenging. A good example is the stories of Abba Poemen:

Some monks came to see Abba Poemen and said to him, "We see some brothers falling asleep during divine worship, should we wake them up?" He replied, "As for me when I

---

[68] Merton op. cit. p.19.
[69] Early Fathers op. cit. p.127.

see a brother who is falling asleep during the Office, I lay head on my knees and let him rest".[70]

Abba Poemen, though, models not simply a gentle loving heart but also the example of the gospel teaching in another story when he is asked to give advice about anger:

> A brother asked Abba Poemen, "What does it mean to be angry with your brother without cause?"[71] He said if your brother hurts you by his arrogance and you are angry with him because of this, that is getting angry without cause. If he pulls out your right eye and cuts off your right hand and you get angry with him, that is getting angry without cause. But if he cuts you off from God, then you have every right to be angry with him.[72]

Abba Poemen illustrates in this story not only ironic humour but also that humour and humility can serve to challenge the contemplative seeker to go deeper into the relationship with a loving heart to know the depths of the love of Jesus. Cutting off from God being the fundamental alienation of human society which the contemplative discerns in the ongoing and foundational relationship of silent prayer. Abba Poemen recognises that the loving heart is of supreme importance, the primacy of silent prayer taking precedence of all else and acknowledging in humility the love of Christ, which is always with us.

---

[70] Williams op. cit. p.30.
[71] Matthew 5:21.
[72] Williams op. cit. p.31.

It is this humility in Christ which allows even the most holy and devout still to understand the close need for that relationship to be with Christ, which is ongoing and can never be broken. Abba Pastor speaks of this central relationship: 'A man must breathe humility just as he inhales and exhales the air'.[73] Abba Alonius is just as clear when he advises, 'Humility is the land where God wants us to go'.[74] Again, Abba Poemen gives a word which challenges his questioner's assumption and, in humility, turns the question around:

> A brother questioned Abba Poeman saying, "If I see my brother sinning, should I hide the fact?" The old man replied, "At the moment when we hid a brother's fault, God hides our own. At the moment when we reveal a brother's fault, God reveals our own".[75]

Therefore, humility is the central characteristic of those who have the loving heart of Jesus. The 'prayer of the heart' in the Eastern tradition is an expression of the centrality of humility in the life of the contemplative.

Often less well-known but equally worth reading is the advice of the desert ammas. Best known of these and a contemporary of Antony is Amma Syncletica, who reminded those who questioned her that 'neither vigils nor any kind of suffering are able to save, only true humility can do that'.[76] Syncletica was a very rich woman who inherited her parents' wealth. Inspired by the example of Antony, though, she gave away all she had and

---

[73] Merton op. cit. p.53.
[74] Ibid., p.53.
[75] Williams op. cit. p.29.
[76] Earle op. cit. p.47.

lived among the tombs close to Alexanderia. Although she was an ascetic herself, she did not advocate this path for all; rather, she taught moderation after the example of Christ and recognised that the loving heart of Jesus was known through a humble life. Mary Earle, in commenting on the example of humility among the earliest ammas, writes of their distinctive contemplative life:

> Amma Theodora's sayings emphasize self-discipline and humility, stressing the creative tension between love and mercy of God and the human responsibility to respond to the gift of that love and mercy. She also emphasized living in peace with oneself. To live in peace with ourselves, we first need to practice humility.[77]

Humility for the earliest ammas is distinctive in a way of coming to know who we truly are as God's creation. Moderation in everything is key to the way of humility, which they understand as being key to living in the loving heart of Jesus. Amma Dorotheos advises, 'Courage stands in the middle between cowardice and foolhardiness; humility in the middle between arrogance and severity. Modesty is a mean between timidity and boldness'.[78] Whilst humility itself is perceived as giving the strength to overcome everything in the name of Christ, 'humility protects the soul from all the passions and also from every temptation'.[79]

The witness of the earliest ammas is therefore consistent with the teaching of the abbas, yet at the same time each brings a

---

[77] Ibid p.47.
[78] Ibid., p.52.
[79] Ibid., p.53.

distinctive nuance to the importance of humility for the loving heart. For the ammas, it is about not simply being in Christ; rather, it is fundamentally that we are all created in love by God, and, in humility, heaven and earth meet. The contemplative comes to recognise the great truth of our existence that we do not bring ourselves into being, nor do we make creation. Rather, we are birthed of God; in him we live and move and have our being.

For the Eastern Church, Antony is one of the four 'Fathers of the Church'. John Chrysostom, one of these fathers, was born in the fourth century, but it is unlikely that he would ever have met Antony. However, John Chrysostom was familiar with the conferences of John Cassian, whom he indeed could have met in person. In the conferences, John Chrysostom would have read of the centrality of humility in the contemplative's life.
'Humility of soul helps more than everything else; without it no one can overcome lewdness or any other sin'.[80] Cassian reads and repeats the advice of Antony and the earliest desert teachers, stressing the priority of humility for all who seek the loving heart, and his teaching is repeated by John Chrysostom:

> Let it be known to you that if in your life you have mastered every virtue and every good deed such as mercy, prayer, fast, and other virtues but have no humility in you, your toil will be in vain. For humility in all these virtues is the solid foundation. Without it, we cannot master any of the virtues and all these virtues will become impure, filthy, and

---

[80] Cassian op. cit. p.50.

discarded before God because they were not sown with humility and love.[81]

Humility is therefore not to be understood as a virtue but rather as core to the contemplative's relationship with the loving heart of Jesus.

In Antony, we come to see that the contemplative path is the way of love. This love is about charity. This is well illustrated by the story of the generous gift of a nobleman recorded in the *Verba Seniorum*:

A great noble whom nobody knew came to Scete bringing with him gold, and he asked the abba to hand it out to the monks. The abba replied, "The brothers don't need any of this". The nobleman though insisted and would not take "no" for an answer; so the nobleman placed the basket of gold down at the entrance to the church. He said, "Those who want some can help themselves". But no one touched any of the gold, and some did not even look at it. Then the abba said to the nobleman, "The Lord has accepted your offering, go now and give it to the poor".[82]

Whilst love is about charity, it is not simply about giving; it is rather about knowing that our lives are held in love. This story reminds us that these earliest contemplatives knew of the importance of the latter as well as the former. Many of those who had gold placed before them didn't even look, for they

---

[81] *On Living Simply*, Homilies of St John Chrysostom, Liguori Publications, 1997, p.42,
[82] Merton op. cit. p.72.

knew something greater in their lives – the loving heart of Christ, in which their souls were constantly held.

Antony himself urges those who seek God to acknowledge their dependence upon the love:

> God's providence controls the universe. It is present everywhere. Providence is the sovereign logos of God, imprinting form on the unformed materiality of the world, making and fashioning all things. Matter could not have acquired an articulated structure were it not for the directing power of the logos, who is the image, intellect, wisdom and providence of God.[83]

Love is therefore where the soul resides in the loving heart of the divine; this is perhaps acknowledged in prayer in the conscious mind, but also for Antony it is our ever-present reality whether we are conscious or unconscious of this love. In his 170 sayings in *On the Character of Men*, Antony ends with this wonderful description of how the soul is held by God at all times:

> 'When you go to bed with a contented mind, recall the blessings and generous providence of God; be filled with holy thoughts and great joy. Then, while your body sleeps, your soul will keep watch; the closing of your eyes will bring you a true vision of God; your silence will be pregnant with sanctity, and in your sleep, you will continue consciously to glorify the God of all with the full strength of your soul.[84]

---

[83] *The Philokalia*, volume 1, op. cit. p.353.
[84] Ibid., p.355.

The loving heart is in the contemplative who seeks Christ in silence and humbly knows him in love. Jesus weeps at the tomb of Lazarus; he shows the great heart of love which he shares with God. The divine character is revealed in the loving heart of Jesus. Those who journeyed into the desert inspired by Antony knew this great truth from the gospel of John, revealed to them in silent prayer and which they discern in the lives of others who too sought the stillness and silence of love. This love demanded complete inner transformation; to be turned inwards was to be opened outwards. The loving heart causes us in contemplation to become the person we love; we are changed as we come to know the divine that dwells within and recognise the love of Jesus within the heart of those around us. In this recognition of our self, our life becomes part of something greater, we are held in love, we know that love, and it is this love that is always present, always near and always holding us close.

Chapter Five: Loving Life

Jesus said to them, 'Very truly, I tell you, I am the gate for the sheep. All who came before me are thieves and bandits; but the sheep did not listen to them. I am the gate. Whoever enters by me will be saved, and will come in and go out and find pasture. The thief comes only to steal and kill and destroy. I came that they may have life, and have it abundantly. I am the good shepherd. The good shepherd lays down his life for the sheep'.[85]

Antony didn't go into the desert to escape life but rather to embrace living in its fullest sense. Exploring silence is never an escape. The prayer of the heart requires us to be attentive to God. By seeking the divine love within us, we open our inner lives and become as vulnerable as any child. If we live in this way and place our lives before God, then we come to know his goodness in all we say and do. We should understand Antony's example in the context of the words of Jesus: 'I have come that they may have life'. This is what Antony sought, and this is what each of us seeks in our life's journey. To be obedient to love is therefore the only thing that matters. For if God is love and if we seek His life in all its fullness, only in loving life can we come to fully explore the mystery of the Trinity.

Athanasius tells us of Antony's character, which embraced life, extolling his piety, vitality, energy and passion:

> Antony, the man of God, who from youth to so great an age preserved a uniform zeal for the discipline, and neither through old age was subdued by the desire of costly food,

---

[85] John 10:7–11.

not through the infirmity of his body. His eyes were undimmed and quite sound and he saw clearly. He remained strong both in hands and feet; and while all men were using various foods, and various garments, he appeared more cheerful and of greater strength. And the fact that his fame has been blazoned everywhere; that all regard him with wonder, and that those who had never seen him long for him, is clear proof of his virtue and God's love of his soul. For not from writings, not from worldly wisdom, nor through any art, was Antony renowned, but solely from his piety towards God. That this was the gift of God no one will deny.[86]

Athanasius, although not writing a biography, gives us an impression of the impact that Antony made on others. It was not simply his teaching and advice that impressed but also the way he lived his life. Antony's greatest gift is his piety. It is the faithfulness of life to the loving heart of Jesus he reads about in the gospel of John, which transformed his life and made him an example for others to follow.

Athanasius also praises Antony's discernment:

For this was the wonderful thing in Antony's discipline, that, as I said before, having the gift of discerning spirits, he recognized their movements, and was not ignorant whither any one of them turned his energy and made his attack. And not only was he not deceived by them himself, but cheering those who were troubled with doubts, he taught them how to

---

[86] Anathanasius op. cit. p.50.

defeat their plans, telling them of the weakness and craft of those who possessed them.[87]

Here, Athanasius reminds us, as his readers, of the faithful life of Antony, which gives him the clarity to seek beyond the immediate and to discern clearly God's purposes and the power of evil. In Antony's time, he sees the work of evil personified in demons and the devil. Of course, we too see evil in people: either the notorious dictators of the twentieth century or the criminal serial killers of society. We also see the demons that many ordinary people carry, which inhibit and ruin their lives, past hatreds, addictions or controlling desires. What is thought-provoking in Antony's witness is that he does not discount them, as so often we do, and holds on to the hope that each of these wicked persons is also created by God.

For the contemplative, the power of evil to threaten the fullness of life is ever-present. Antony helps us to understand that life can never be lived to the full unless we recognise that everything is in God's hand; he abides in all things. Some significant parts of the hagiography written by Athanasius consist of Antony's battles with demons, but this should not be understood in simplistic dualistic terms. Thomas Merton points to the significance of these cosmic battles:

> Antony achieved the faithful life after some long and somewhat spectacular contests with demons. But in the end, he concluded that not even the devil was purely evil, since God could not create evil, and all God's works are good. It

---

[87] Ibid., p.47.

may come as a surprise to learn that Antony, of all people, thought that the devil had some good in him.[88]

Antony was rooted in the gospel of John and recognised that the goodness of God was in all things from the beginning to the end and discerned that goodness all around him. The practice of silent prayer turned him inwards to know the interior love of God dwelling within his soul, which then turned him outwards to recognise the divine love in others, bringing all together in a community of sacred unity found in the loving heart of Jesus. He also expressed this not simply in his words but also by his example of a faithful life.

So what kind of life did these earliest desert fathers and mothers lead? In later centuries, there are many extreme examples of hermits living on the top of pillars, but in the fourth century, the abbas and ammas lived simple lives. Antony himself set a pattern of a simple life, simply lived. Famously, the advice given by many desert teachers is for the novice who sought the contemplative life to 'go to their cell and that will teach everything'. This may suggest a very Spartan existence, but on the contrary, their lifestyles would be envied by many in our modern world. They built their cells of two or three rooms on the edge of the desert, often within sight of the sea and with access to fresh water. They would have gardens attached and grow a range of vegetables and fruit. They kept animals often like Antony: chickens or other small domesticated animals. They would often swap or exchange food with others as well as feed the destitute or widowed and orphaned. They didn't live together physically but associated with one another, often having their cells within sight of each other and would warn

---

[88] Merton op. cit. p.21.

their neighbours of bandits operating in their district. Some would support themselves and one another through crafts, making wool, weaving cloth, creating baskets or mats, but acts of charity and hospitality always took precedence. They would travel to seek advice from the most famous of abbas and ammas. Thomas Merton sums up the lives of these contemplatives as follows:

> The countless sayings which bear witness to this warm-hearted friendliness should be sufficient to take care of accusations that these people were harsh. Indeed, there was more real love, understanding and kindliness in the desert than in the cities.[89]

One of the other Fathers of the Church, John Chrysostom, gives us an insight into this practical wisdom which encouraged Christians in the fourth century to live faithfully. He famously says in a homily:

> 'I am always encouraging you, and I am not going to stop encouraging you, to pay attention to what is said here in church, but also, when you are at home, to continue constantly in the practice of reading the divine Scriptures. And don't let anyone make excuses like, "I'm too busy with politics". "I'm a businessman". "I'm a skilled worker. I must get on with my job". "I've got a wife". "I'm raising children". "I'm responsible for a household". In other words, "I'm a lay person; it's not my business to read the scriptures. I'll leave that to professional Christians like monks, nuns, priests and theology students". What are you saying? It's not your business to pay attention to the scriptures because you

---

[89] Ibid., p.16.

are distracted by thousands of concerns? But that's the very reason why you need to read them! The more worries you have, the more you need the scriptures to keep you going![90]

These desert teachers were of the world but not conformed to it; their advice often challenged conventional wisdom and the easy compromises of the world.

In the fourth century, the word 'paganus' in Latin literally meant a simple person, a rural rustic, or, as we might say, a 'country yokel'. 'Pagan' didn't mean 'unbeliever' – rather more an 'idiot'. This demonstrates the view of the fourth-century church leadership after the establishment of the Imperial Church; the cities were thought of as the spiritual homes of Christianity. During the fourth century, the great councils of the church took place in these great cities in Nicaea, Chalcedon and Laodicea. The sponsoring cities of the four gospels which are included in the New Testament canon – Antioch, Rome, Ephesus and Alexandria – demonstrate the powerful influence of these great cities. Antony, in leaving the city to go to the desert, made a bold statement about faith and the faithful life. He saw in the city the hypocrisy of power and wealth corrupting the faith. He believed that the faithful life was impossible among the political compromises of living under the empire's corrupting influence. It is ironic that history remembers Constantine the Great as the first Christian emperor, but at the time Antony regarded the new empire as simply another form of persecution and enslavement to the imperial authority. Liberation was key and freedom in Christ central to his understanding of living out the gospel in the loving heart of Jesus. Thomas Merton understands this to be Antony's greatest legacy to us; he believed that this tradition

---

[90] Chrysostom op. cit. p.109.

was held in the fourth century by ordinary men and women. It was their ordinariness that was key. Antony came to the desert to be himself, truly and authentically indwelt by the divine light, liberated and freed from the evil of the city. Merton extols this faithful life: 'Let it suffice for me to say that we need to learn from these saints of the fourth century how to ignore prejudice, defy compulsion and strike out fearlessly into the unknown'.[91]

A hallmark of the lives of the desert fathers and mothers was their self-deprecating compassion; often they would use simple actions or parables to call into question harsh teaching or treatment. A story of Abba Moses serves to illustrate this point:

> There was a brother at Scetis who had committed a fault. So, a meeting was called and Abba Moses was invited. He refused to go. Word was sent to him, "They are all waiting for you". So, Abba Moses got up and set off; he took a leaky jug and filled it with water and took it with him. The others came to meet him and looking at the jug said, "What is this?" The old man replied, "My sins run out behind me and I cannot see them, yet here I am coming to sit in judgement on the mistakes of somebody else". When they heard this, they called off the meeting.[92]

Living life in all its fullness meant more than an inwards journey into the self; it was also a recognition of the faults and failings that all share in seeking the contemplative way.

In the same vein, Amma Sarah says that 'it is good to give alms for people's sake, even if it is done only to please others,

---

[91] Ibid., p.24.
[92] Williams op. cit. p.29.

through it one can begin to seek to please God'.[93] The desert fathers and mothers needed to care for one another; though they lived separately, they associated communally. In addition, many sought them out in the desert not just to seek God's word but also for hospitality and healing. Amma Sarah's advice expresses an understanding of the variety of reasons behind any charitable gift but recognises all such gifts as pleasing to God. Her sayings assume that all seek to please God, and in this view, she is very typical of the desert teachers. They lived their faithful lives, obedient to Christ's command to love and in the belief that this was their vocation.

Athanasius tells us of Antony's final advice to a group of monks. Often his sayings appear to relate to an early understanding of the Trinity. He himself often quoted from John's gospel speaking of God in relationship with the Son and in the power of the Spirit. The doctrines of the church and the canons of scripture were still being formed in Antony's lifetime. Indeed, the arguments were not resolved into the creeds until later; the final form of the canon of New Testament scriptures was agreed forty-six years after his death. In his final messages of advice, he warned against the heresies of the Arians and other heresies. His Trinitarian understanding of the way God abides in us and we in God of course has found a rich home in the contemplatives who followed in his way. Yet it is difficult to accept that Antony himself would have supported the creation of creeds to exclude any believer. The generous heart of his faith is heard in his leaving words to his brethren for the final time. Athanasius recalls:

---

[93] Earle op. cit. p.73.

He as though sailing from a foreign city to his own spoke joyously and exhorted them, "not to grow idle in their labours, nor to become faint in their training, but to live as though dying daily. And as he had said before eagerly to imitate the saints and keep yourselves all the more untainted and observe the traditions of the fathers and chiefly the holy faith in our Lord Jesus Christ, which you have learned from scripture, and of which you have often been put in mind by me".[94]

Athanasius tells his readers that Antony died at the age of 105. Other sources suggest that he lived until his mid-nineties. Whatever his age, he must have lived a long life spanning the persecutions of Diocletian and to have seen the Imperial Christian Church in the fourth century. We can be certain of the year of his death in 356 as it is attested in many ancient sources. It does seem that many of the earliest desert teachers lived long lives. Whilst it's tempting to believe that this may be a symbolic record of old age pointing to their wisdom, more recent archaeological evidence would suggest that many did live to their eighties or nineties. Given that they lived separately, there is evidence that they were less susceptible to disease and plague. Their diets were naturally nutritious, and the consumption of large quantities of fish provided a plentiful supply of natural oils and vitamins. It is not difficult to assume that they lived long lives.

So what is Antony's relevance to us? What do the desert fathers and mothers have to contribute to the contemplative tradition? Well, their influence, as we shall see, was considerable. Not only is their teaching and advice alluded to by Augustinians and

---

[94] Anathanasius op. cit. p.48.

Benedictines; their pattern of praying was also influential for the Irish monastic mission of the fifth century, and their mysticism inspired Francis, Teresa and Ignatius in turn. Whilst other contemplatives who played a vital part in our Western tradition seem to have had little direct influence from Antony, we can recognise in the words of George Fox, for example, much that would be common to the desert tradition in the priority of John's gospel. Over the past century, though, Antony and his writing have once again become central to contemporary Christian contemplatives. Over and over again, we read advice on the contemplative life, which has resonances from the desert teachers. In the coming chapters, this teaching will be drawn from the writing of Martin Laird, Thomas Keating, Cynthia Bourgeault, John O'Donohue, David Adam, Ray Simpson, J P Newell, John Main, Laurence Freeman, Richard Rohr, Sarah Bachelard, Maggie Ross, Christine Valens Paintner, Brother Roger and many more.

The importance of Antony for contemporary contemplatives cannot be overstated. His influence has often been ignored or relegated to a minor footnote of history. Rather his teaching is foundational to our understanding of contemplation. As we come in the final section of this book to ask what being a contemplative means in our daily lives, Antony can still speak to us in a number of ways. His example of being obedient to love. Demonstrating silence as stillness in loving prayer. His turning inwards to be turned outwards into the community of the loving heart of Jesus shows us the faithful life, lived in all its fullness.

Chapter Six: Silent Land

The foundation of every land is silence, where God simply and perpetually gives Himself. – Martin Laird

Augustine of Hippo was born two years before Antony died. Their lives overlapped, and Augustine knew of Antony's teaching when he came to faith, and it appears to have greatly influenced him later in life, being fundamental to his writings.

The rule of Augustine of Hippo dates from around the year 400. It was popularised by the Norman influence across Western Europe in the eleventh century. The growth of towns, increasing literacy and more stable forms of regional government meant that many sought a more detached form of Christian community not tainted by the world. Allied to this was the shock to medieval Europe of the attack on Jerusalem and the Islamic control of Christian holy sites, which gave rise to the Crusades. Although Christian pilgrims were not prevented from visiting the Holy Land and Christianity was respected by the Muslim overlords, the Pope gave instructions to the princes of Europe to fight a holy war. This atmosphere of increased personal devotion to 'take the cross' is difficult for the modern mind to understand, but it was a powerful influence in creating the prayer houses of England. As well as obviously being the rule for Augustinians, in 1059, at the Lateran Council, 'The Rule of St Augustine'[95] was approved for the use of all clergy. It was

---

[95] *Augustine of Hippo and his Monastic Rule* by George Lawless OSA, OUP, Oxford, 1990.

also the rule chosen for the Dominican, Gilbertine and Premonstratensian orders.

Augustine's rule is quite short and gives an outline of the religious life. It lays down governance covering detachment, acts of charity, community prayers, fasting, care for the infirmed, schooling and silence as well as observes the three principles of chastity, poverty and obedience. It is also collegiate in style, and therefore, the order is understood as a fraternity. Augustine's rule, though, being so short and not being detailed, allowed for a great deal of flexibility in its implementation. At first, these houses of prayer were noted for their simple lifestyle and devotion. Often, the houses would divide the brothers between those who were dedicated entirely to prayer and contemplation and those who were working. Both groups attended the seven offices of the day, but those working in the kitchen, infirmary, school or on the estate were busy keeping the monastery functioning. The other brothers would dedicate themselves entirely to silence, prayer and reflection. In the beginning, there was no division of status between the two groups. Visiting the sites of their abbeys today, it is striking that they chose places of remarkable stillness and peace. The location of their abbeys, though chosen for many reasons, illustrates the centrality of detachment and silence in the Augustinian rule. Though their influence was lost in England at the time of the dissolution of the monasteries, the Augustinian rule continues to offer this way of silence in contemplative prayer.

Martin Laird is perhaps the best-known contemporary Augustinian writer. In his classic book *Into the Silent Land*, Laird explores the necessity of silence to the life of prayer. The beginning of his book is a manifesto for silent prayer:

We are built for contemplation. Communion with God in the silence of the heart is a God-given capacity, like the rhododendron's capacity to flower, the fledgling's for flight and the child's for self-forgetful abandon and joy.[96]

For Augustinians, then, silent prayer was not about technique and a style of praying. Rather, silence was 'the homeland of the soul'. To have such a rich Augustinian heritage in the sites of so many pre-Reformation abbeys speaks to us still of their priority of prayer, a priority which, in their understanding, springs from our essential God-given nature rather than something that we adopt or copy for ourselves.

Martin Laird describes the essential nature of the Augustinian understanding of prayer when he writes, 'There are two contemplative practices of fundamental importance in the Christian tradition: the practice of stillness (also called meditation, still prayer, contemplative prayer) and the practice of watchfulness or awareness'.[97] For Laird, 'God is our homeland', and these two practices of prayer are typical of the Augustinian detachment from the world as the soul 'rests' in God. Stillness and watchfulness are the keys to Augustinian prayer. These twin practices are not understood as a route to find God; rather, they are the experience of being with God. This is a worldview that the earliest monks would have known and understood when he says:

An ancient Christian view is that the foundation of every land is silence, where God simply and perpetually gives

---

[96] *Into the Silent Land* by Martin Laird, DLT, London, 2006, p.1.
[97] Ibid., 5.

Himself. This self-gift is manifested in the creation, in the people of God and their inspired (if stumbling) pursuit of a just society, and most fully, in the Christian view of things, in Jesus Christ. This is the homeland, to which every spiritual pilgrim is constantly being called, called home, as St Augustine says, "From the noise that is around us to the joys that are silent. Why do we rush about looking for God who is here at home with us, if all we want is to be with him".[98]

Laird grounds his writings about the practice of silent prayer in the example of Antony and the desert teachers. He notes that for them and us, 'Jesus is the prime example of the practice of contemplation'.[99] He notes how Abba Evagrius in the conference record by Cassian cites Jesus himself as the prime example of the contemplative life and writes of Jesus being tempted in the wilderness as instructive for all those who seek the path of stillness and silent prayer. The devil distracts the contemplative Jesus with temptations of worldly pleasure, fame and fortune. Distractions to take him away from the path of a true relationship with the divine. For Augustine, Jesus is the anchor of contemplation; this relationship holds the contemplative fast amid the challenges and temptations of the world. Martin Laird uses the quotation from Abba John Climacus to stress this point: 'Let the remembrance of Jesus be with your every breath. Then indeed you will appreciate the value of stillness'.[100] For Augustinians, therefore, silence is central to our relationship in Christ. Laird again quotes Evagrius when it comes to the practice of contemplation: 'Let us still and

---

[98] Ibid., p.6.
[99] *Sunlit Absence* by Martin Laird, OUP, New York, 2011, p.13.
[100] Ibid., p.14.

keep our attention fixed within ourselves'.[101] For Laird, this is God's gift to us in grace; notably he uses John 17 to express this belief:

> The grace of salvation, the grace of Christian wholeness that flowers in silence, dispels the illusion of separation. For when the mind is brought to stillness, and all our strategies of acquisition have dropped, a deeper truth presents itself: we are and have always been one with God and we are all one in God.[102]

Whilst Thomas Keating as a Cistercian is strictly a Benedictine, the contemporary 'centring prayer' movement he founded has more in common with Augustine. Keating traces the origins of the understanding of contemplation to the Greek Fathers in his foundational book *Intimacy with God*,[103] defining contemplation as 'the knowledge of God that is impregnated with love',[104] for Keating also looked back to the desert teachers who spoke of the purpose of silent prayer being to rest in God. This resting he defines as:

> The state is not the suspension of all activity, but the reduction of many acts and reflections to a single act or thought to sustain one's consent to God's presence and action at the depths of one's being during the time of prayer.[105]

---

[101] Ibid., p.15.

[102] *Into the Silent Land,* op. cit. p.16.

[103] *Intimacy with God* by Thomas Keating, Crossroads, 2009.

[104] Ibid., p.123.

[105] Ibid., p.123.

The result of this resting in God is to experience a personal love of Christ. So, for Keating, it is as much Christ's humanity that speaks to us in contemplation, as well as the divine life with it. He comments:

> Once faith has revealed the mystery of Christ's humanity, one's attention during prayer is absorbed by the presence of the divine Person who dwells within it. One returns to daily life with this transformed consciousness, manifesting the fruits of the Spirit and the Beatitudes.[106]

Cynthia Bourgeault, as part of the centring prayer movement, sees Jesus as the key person of the contemplative life: 'It seems safe to assume that Jesus was a contemplative, by which I mean that the intentional alteration between contemplation and action is one of the fundamental rhythms of his being'. [107] For Bourgeault, the recovery of the desert wisdom, which for her was a discovery made through the writings of Thomas Merton, was key in exploring Christian meditation. For her, 'the cornerstone both in prayer and daily life, was the practice of attention'.[108] The practice of centring prayer requiring attention to a word to lead into silence is inspired by the discipline of the desert writings. She herself concludes:

> As Abba Macarius teaches, in what could well be seen as a fourth-century forerunner of centring prayer: "there is no need to make long discourses; it is enough stretch out one's

---

[106] Ibid., p.129.
[107] *Centreing Prayer and Inner Awakening* by Cynthia Bourgeault, Cowley, 2004, p.59.
[108] Ibid., p.61.

hands and say, Lord as you will and as you know, have mercy. And as the conflict grows fiercer, say Lord help!"[109]

For Augustinians and those who follow centring prayer, contemplation is about keeping the discipline of attentive silence. Christian prayer is thought of as being cataphatic and apophatic. Cataphatic refers to those forms that we are so used to in Western churches, the noise and wordiness of public worship and our prayer books. Apophatic is the total emptying of thoughts and distractions to find the purity of prayer within. The increasing popularity of apophatic prayer, as demonstrated by the growing numbers of contemplative movements, is causing the desert teaching to be revisited and to speak again to us. Sometimes criticised in the modern church for being narcissistic, Keating explains clearly how this form of apophatic prayer brings us deeper into communion with one another. In this passage, he seems to be expressing something of Antony's understanding of loving community:

> Centering Prayer comes out of life of God moving within us. It establishes us in a deepening relationship with Christ. Begun in the prayerful reading of scripture and other devotions and especially in the sacraments, our relationship with Christ moves to new depths and to new levels of intimacy as we grow in the practice of Centering Prayer. It is also ecclesial in its effects; that is, it bonds us with everyone else in the Mystical Body of Christ and indeed with the whole human family. There is really no such thing as private prayer. We cannot pray at this deep level without including

---

[109] Ibid., p.63.

everyone in the human family, especially those in great need.[110]

For Keating, contemplation is the practice of 'the narrow way that leads to life'. His emphasis is on the work of the Holy Spirit in revealing to us the depth of sacred unity in silent prayer. He understands the transformation of silence to be the work of the Holy Spirit rather than any form of human psychological technique. Summing up the impact of centring prayer, he concludes:

> Thus, the essence of the contemplative path is the trusting and loving faith by which God both elevates the human person and purifies the conscious and unconscious obstacles in us that oppose the values of the gospel and the work of the Spirit.[111]

For Bourgeault also, silent prayer is a narrow path but one which is liberating leading to life fully lived. She doesn't see the contemplative path as one which leads the person to live separately or apart but rather like the desert teachers to live ordinary lives, where both prayer and life are experienced authentically. Centring prayer is therefore not a technique to be learned but rather a framework for an ordinary life to be lived. She comes to this understanding of the hidden power of prayer in this simple conclusion:

> The reality is that God is always present, and we're the ones who are absent! We hide in the cataphatic: in our noise, our stories, our self-talking, our busyness. Silence is useful in

---

[110] Keating, pp.167–8.
[111] Ibid., p.131.

that it takes away the evasions; it forces us to befriend our own consciousness and stop running from our own shadows. Once that willingness has been found, the willingness simply to endure ourselves in the present moment, then the external conditions of silence become much less important.[112]

For Laird, contemplation is a gift of God. He quotes Augustine in the belief that silent prayer is something we experience in relationship with the divine rather than learn in a technique: 'While God made you without you, he doesn't justify you without you'.[113] This is God's true nature; it is something that Antony knew. 'God is always self-giving; it is a question of removing the obstacles that make it difficult to receive this self-gift. This receptivity is what contemplative practice cultivates'. [114] Laird teaches that silent prayer should be understood as three doors through which the soul passes as it develops an ever-deeper relationship with the divine within. This image of the door being directly related to John 10 verse 9 again echoes the priority of this gospel for contemplation. Laird sums up this movement of the soul in silent prayer:

We realise that what beholds this vast and flowing whole is also the whole. We see that these thoughts and feelings that have plagued us, clouded our vision, seduced us, entertained us, have no substance. They too are a manifestation of the vastness in which they appear.[115]

---

[112] Bourgeault op. cit. p.157.
[113] *Into the Silent Land,* op. cit. p.54.
[114] Ibid., p.56.
[115] Ibid., p.93.

This is the peace of Christ, which the desert teachers called resting in Christ. He appears to echo some of the teachings of Antony in likening contemplative prayer to sailing a boat, using a practical example to sum up the practice of silent prayer:

> A sailor cannot produce the necessary wind that moves the boat. A sailor practices sailing skills that harness the gift of wind that brings the sailor home, but there is nothing the sailor can do to make the wind blow. And so it is with contemplative practice, not a technique, but a skill. The skill required is interior silence.[116]

The primacy of silent prayer as expressed by Antony in the fourth century still resonates with contemplatives. Laird, Keating and Bourgeault, who encourage contemporary contemplatives to explore silent prayer, are rooted in the tradition of the desert father and mothers. Their insights still speak to us and remind us from John's gospel in the way of apophatic prayer that the discipline of silence drives away distractions and fixes our attention to the love of Christ within.

---

[116] Ibid., p.4.

Chapter Seven: Living Like a River

I would love to live
Like a river flows,
Carried by the surprise
Of its own unfolding.[117] *– John O'Donohue*

Ninian was born four years after Antony died and, in his community at Whithorn, brought the desert teachings into the life of the church in Britain. Ninian was born into a world where the Roman Empire was Christian but facing financial and organisational challenges. The external threats were becoming more pressing, and the old certainties were rapidly being lost. Ninian was perhaps born in Galloway, north of the Roman Wall; his birthplace is assumed to be there because he was said to have returned to his home when he founded his community at Whithorn. Ninian travelled to Rome for his Christian education and ordination and return via the Martin of Tours community at Marmoutier. It is not known exactly when he came to Whithorn, but it would have been close to the beginning of the fifth century, just as the Pax Romana was about to break down in Britain.

Ninian's community flourished at Whithorn, drawing admirers and students from across Europe. At Whithorn in 451, the earliest known Christian inscription in Britain was carved on a gravestone; who Latinus was and why he was important enough to have his own stone are unclear. What is obvious, though, are the opening words of his inscription: 'Te Deum laudemus'. Here

---

[117] *Benedictus* by John O'Donohue , Bantam Press, London, 2007, p.119.

was a lively Christian community where those who died were celebrated for their faith. It seems likely that Cumbria was the home of Patrick. There are several places associated with Ireland's patron saint in the county. He was kidnapped probably a few years after Ninian had set up his community at Whithorn. The beginning of the fifth century was a time of intense raiding from the tribes of Ulster as the coast was no longer defended by the Roman fleet. It seems entirely reasonable that Patrick, as the son of a Christian deacon, Calpornius, was snatched as a slave of the U Neill clan from a beach on the Solway Firth overlooked by the hill to which his ashes would return in 461, now known as Aspatria (an abbreviation of its ancient name 'The Ashes of St Patrick'). Patrick's experience of slavery brought him to a personal revelation of faith similar to Antony's during his time locked away in the Egyptian graves. John O'Donohue comments:

> His physical slavery releases him into a life of inner liberation. His captors only controlled his tasks and location, but they never got near the eternal spring of his young mind. In this awful experience of alienation and exile, he discovers God as his anam cara, (the friend of the soul). An ancient affinity and belonging awakened in the anam-cara relationship. In your anam-cara you discover the Other in whom your heart could be at home.[118]

Ninian and Patrick were both educated in Rome. They were ordained in Rome and held commissions as missionaries. They were evangelists of the Christian Church. Many histories speak foolishly of the Roman Church, the British Church and the

---

[118] *The Confession of Saint Patrick,* translated by John Skinner, Doubleday, New York, 1998, viii.

Celtic Church. All these terms are inventions of later generations. Ninian and Patrick recognised only one Church, united by one baptism, a community of disciples of one Lord and faithful to the books of the good news of Jesus. These books, which were for the first time authorised as sacred scripture by the great council of Laodicea in 363, were known to Ninian and Patrick. Of all the new books of the Bible, though, the one simply titled 'According to John' was regarded as the most important. Antony the Great had died a few years earlier, but his influence on the early Constantine Church of the fourth century was immense. Antony's devotion to Jesus as presented in the gospel of John was fundamental to the prayer tradition of the desert fathers and mothers. In turn, the conversations with John Cassian with the abbas and ammas of the desert tradition were held dear by St Martin at Marmoutier. Ninian not only brought with him from Marmoutier the stonemasons who built Candida Casa (Latin for 'white house', from which the present name Whithorn comes) but also a way of praying in creation rooted in Antony's teaching. Antony told all those who came to him in the desert to be obedient to the command of Jesus that he knew from John's gospel 'to love one another'. He was for both Ninian and Patrick their father in faith.

Ninian and Patrick created the distinctive pattern of Christian community which a century later was the most significant feature of the Christian Church in Britain. Communities were founded on the Irish pattern in the land of the Picts by Mungo, who was known as Kentigern in England. The communities of Ninian, Patrick and Kentigern all followed a similar pattern. Ian Bradley notes that these communities had a lot in common with the desert teachers:

> In many respects Celtic monastic life was based on the monasticism which flourished in Egypt and Palestine in the

fourth and fifth centuries. The desert fathers pioneered both the eremitic (solitary) and cenobitic (communal) strands so often existed side by side in Irish communities.[119]

These communities were basically stockade settlements built on or nearby rivers and lakes. The roundhouses provided communal living for families and individuals. Like the modern-day Coptic religious, the only indication that any individual was a monk, nun, priest or bishop was in the style of clothing and a shaven forehead. The distinctive feature of these Christian settlements was the central building, which served as church, a scriptorium/school as well as an infirmary/guest house. This building was always aligned east to west, and in the church, there was one small window high in the east gable end. The members of the community waited patiently in darkness every Sunday morning for the first light of dawn to appear through the east window to signal the start of the Eucharist after the example of Mary Magdalene, who met Jesus at the first light in the resurrection story from John's gospel. This model of community was remarkably successful.

Community life, though, was rooted in contemplation. The pattern of daily prayer noted in so many of the saints' lives was of silent prayer in God's creation. Cuthbert is an example from the seventh century. The story of him entering the channel of water between the priory and a small island is told many times. He allows the tide to bring the water above his shoulders, whilst silently he meditates. The stories are so well known that even to this day, the small island is known as St Cuthbert's Island. This is a thread that runs through all the descriptions of the early

---

[119] *Colonies of Heaven* by Ian Bradley, DLT, London, 2000, p.11.

saints' lives. Patrick tells of praying silently in creation during his slavery in Ireland, David standing in the waves of the Welsh coast, Mungo in the waters of the Clyde, Columba kneeling at the water's edge on Iona as the tide came in and so many more. All this practice appears to come from Ninian, who read of the desert teaching with Martin in the words of Cassian and in the sayings of Antony. Ray Simpson reflects on the importance of the desert connection:

> Martin founded a Christ-like community at Tours, which influenced many visitors from Britain. Certainly, there was a new vision which began to grip the Christians in the Celtic fringe of the west. It was the vision of holy men and women creating communities of light in the eastern deserts.[120]

This engagement, though, was not only in one direction. The Irish communities gave shelter to Christians from persecution in Europe and then later sent missionaries. In the fifth century, the Book of Leinster also mentions seven monks who visited from Egypt. As a result, the inspiration of Antony is clear, as Nora Chadwick reflects:

> We must postulate a strong intellectual influence operating on our islands from the east Mediterranean. There can be little doubt that it was mainly through books that knowledge came to Ireland from the Eastern Church, and that it was through books that they acquired their anchorite discipline from the East.[121]

---

[120] *Exploring Celtic Spirituality* by Ray Simpson, Kevin Mayhew, Suffolk, 2004, p.52.
[121] *The Age of the Saints in the Early Celtic Church* by Nora Chadwick, OUP, 1961, p.51.

The influence of Antony and the contemplative path is most striking in the origins of Celtic spirituality. J Philip Newell notices the connection between Antony's teaching of the two books of God's revelation, scripture and creation, in the earliest spirituality:

> The illuminated manuscripts and the continuing themes of Celtic spirituality that they conveyed were echoed by the great high-standing crosses of the Celtic church. In the St John's and St Martin's crosses of Iona dating from the eighth and ninth centuries, creation and scripture are in separable. The orb at the centre of the cross, representing the sun and light of the world, and the scripture and nature images carved on opposite sides of the cross express the desire to hold together the revelation of God in creation and the revelation of God in the Bible. They reflect the practice of learning for the living Word of God in nature as well as in the scriptures.[122]

The twin sources of revelation for the desert teachers are held in unity by Celtic spirituality and have been explored by various writers in this tradition. It is one of the most noticeable features of Celtic spirituality. Dun Scotus expressed this memorably by saying that Christ walked on earth with two shoes: one of creation and one of scriptures. George MacLeod, in refounding the Iona community in 1938, often in his prayers and poems uses the imagery of creation to reflect on revealed truth from scripture; the following lines from 'Glory in the Grey' exemplify this beautifully:

---

[122] *Listening for the Heartbeat of God* by J Philip Newell, SPCK, London, 2008, p.34.

Almighty God, Redeemer:
Even as with our bodies, so also with our souls.
Redeemer, Christ:
Sunshine and storm, mist and greyness
Eddy round our inner lives.
But as we trace the pattern, looking back,
We know that both darkness and light have been of Thine ordaining
For our own soul's health.
Thy constant care in all, and everywhere,
Is manifest.[123]

A contemporary Celtic poet, Kenneth Steven, also brings together these twin themes and sees the balance in them. In his poem 'The Three Days', he uses creation imagery to bring the meaning for us of Jesus upon the cross through the despair of Mary:

His face, she saw his face, her son
the son she'd brought into a stable
shining with bright rain and blood in rivers
and how his head slipped forwards, finished
his shoulders torn like wings,
like angel wings,
broken now for ever by the weight
of this last loss of God.[124]

Whilst the pattern of the Ninian–Patrick style of Irish monastic communities have much in common with the desert

---

[123] *The Whole Earth Shall Cry Glory* by George MacLeod, Wild Goose Publications, 2006, p.21.
[124] *Evensong* by Kenneth Steven, SPCK, London, 2011, p.43.

contemplatives, there are differences. Bradley comments on this fundamentally different context of the fifth- to seventh-century development in Britain:

> There was one key difference between the two traditions. Whereas the monks in the desert communities generally sought and practiced radical separation from the world, many of the monasteries of the British Isles were intensely involved in the affairs of the world and the lives of the people they served as well as being places of withdrawal and sanctuary.[125]

Antony retreated to the desert because of the hypocrisy of the Imperial Church; in Merton's words, the desert teachers were anarchists. For Ninian and Patrick, their communities were the centres of not just faith but also of learning. Therefore, they were churches, schools, hospitals, farms and educational powerhouses. The sheer quantities of vellum required meant that they had to develop sophisticated techniques of animal husbandry, including regulation of water supplies as well as the manufacture of natural dyes and inks. The number of people required gives credence to the claim of the famous monastery at Clacmanoise on the banks Shannon boasted a community of over two thousand by the turn of the millennium. Though the context was different, the principles learnt through Martin and Cassian remained central.

Of all the functions of the Irish monastic communities, welcoming the stranger was arguably the most important. Hospitality is key in Celtic spirituality, an attribute which is common to the desert teaching. Ray Simpson reminds us:

---

[125] Bradley op. cit. p.11.

Celtic Christians drew inspiration from the desert fathers and mothers with regard to hospitality. They learned from Cassian of the time when he and some friends arrived in Egypt. His friends wondered why the monks they visited had given up their normal practice of fasting. One monk explained: "Fasting is something I do all the time, but it is my choice. But to love is not a matter of choice. So to offer hospitality to you is to fulfil the law of love; it is to receive Christ. Another brother visited a solitary hermit, and apologised for making him break his rule of fasting and silence. The solitary replied: "My rule is to receive you with hospitality and to send you away in peace".[126]

Cuthbert, whilst setting up the community at Ripon with Wilfred, once had a night-time visitor as guest brother. Hearing a knock on the door in the middle of a snowstorm, Cuthbert went to the outer door and welcomed in a young man who was cold and needing not just warmth but also food. Cuthbert sat him by the fire and gave him some food and then pressed on him to stay, for although the snow had now stopped, he could clearly see his visitor was exhausted. Having made up a bed, he returned only to find the young man gone and the outer door open, and as he looked out, he saw no footprints on the newly fallen snow. This is one of many stories which suggest that the earliest communities are visited by Christ himself or angels. Whatever the truth, the pilgrim, stranger or even poor vagrant was always welcomed, allowing the community to show the loving heart of Christ himself.

---

[126] Simpson op. cit. p.96.

There is something more, though, in hospitality. Stephen Wright, in his pilgrimage book of Kentigern, comments on the importance of pilgrimage for the contemplative: 'It's not so much where we pilgrimage but that we are pilgrimage. The consciousness with which we approach pilgrimage, the desire to make the effort, the intention, the surrender of the will, is of greatest importance. Through prayer and effort in faith, working through scripture, opening to the guidance of the Spirit, all these and more, we come to know that the sacred we seek is within. The outer journey, however long or short, paradoxically takes us deeper inwards'.[127] This theme is central to Celtic spirituality and draws us straight back to Antony. John O'Donohue's poem 'The Unknown Self' picks up these themes:

> So much of what delights and troubles you
> happens on a surface
> you take for granted,
> your mind thinks your life alone,
> your eyes consider air your nearest neighbor,
> yet it seems that a little below your heart
> there houses in you an unknown self.
> It is a self that enjoys contemplative patience
> With all your unfolding expression.
> It has the dignity of the angelic
> That knows you to your roots,
> Always awaiting your deeper befriending
> To take you beyond the threshold of want,
> Where all your diverse strainings
> Can come to wholesome ease[128]

---

[127] *The Kentigern Way* by Stephen Wright, Wild Goose Publications, Iona, 2019.
[128] O'Donohue op. cit. pp.158–9.

John O'Donohue, in expressing the contemporary spirituality which is at the heart of so many modern communities such as Iona, Corrymeela and the Northumbria, demonstrates a way of believing that is deeply rooted in Antony's insights and teaching grounded in John's gospel. He writes:

> There is a quiet light that shines in every heart. It draws no attention to itself though it is always secretly there. It is what illuminates our minds to see beauty, our desire to seek possibility and our hearts to love life. This shy inner light is what enables us to recognise and receive our very presence here as blessing. We enter the world as strangers who all at once become heirs to a harvest of memory, spirit and dream that has long preceded us and will now enfold, nourish and sustain us.[129]

This is the beginning of the contemplative life which is so attractive to so many in what is called 'Celtic spirituality' but which in many ways is the founding spirituality of churches in Britain, rooted in the Ninian-style communities which were first informed of the faith through the teaching of the desert fathers and mothers. There is a prayer from the seventh century of Bishop Colman which sums ups this link he is writing of his own cell at Innishboffin, but in so doing, he takes us back to the fourth century and Antony himself:

I wish, O Son of the living God,
O Ancient, Eternal King,
For a little hut in the wilderness,
That it may be my dwelling
A grey lithe lark to be by its side
A clear pool to wash away my sins

---

[129] O'Donohue op. cit. p.1.

Through the grace of the Holy Spirit.
A pleasant church with linen alter cloth,
A dwelling from God of Heaven;
The shining candles above the pure white scriptures,
This is the husbandry I would take,
I would choose and will not hide it[130]

---

[130] *The Edge of Glory* by David Adam, Triangle, 1985, p.90.

Chapter Eight: Conversion of Life

Listen and attend with the ear of your heart. – St Benedict of Nursia

Benedict's rule is the first pattern of communal religious life created by a Christian leader, unlike Augustine of Hippo's Rule which was devised by his disciples. Born fifty years after Augustine died, Benedict lived in a very different world. Esther de Waal calls it 'a world without landmarks'. Certainly, it was a world in turmoil: the great superpower Rome had fallen, and barbarian tribes were ransacking much of the old empire. The church itself was riven with dispute and arguments. Benedict looked back to Antony of Egypt, who lived nearly two centuries earlier. He looked back to a time when Christianity was rooted in contemplative prayer, in the deserts where the pilgrim was welcomed, and where the scriptures were the inspiration for the faithful. In Benedict's time, the scriptures themselves had become the pawns of political and theological dispute. De Waal notes the humanity of Benedict's rule and how it seems to embody his own personality; she says of his words:

> This is the work of a man who has lived what he is writing about, both in the cave at Subiaco and in the monastic enclosure at Monte Cassino. The consummate wisdom which it shows could have emerged from a long and through assimilation, not simply in his mind but in his whole being.[131]

---

[131] *Seeking God* by Esther de Waal, Canterbury Press, Norwich 199, p.5.

Perhaps because of Benedict's own experience, his rule expresses the two great hallmarks of the Benedictines: 'hospitality' and 'welcoming Christ'. All strangers and pilgrims were to be treated in the same way as Christ entering the house. Quoting St Matthew's gospel, Benedict saw the parable of the sheep and goats as being a literal truth: 'I was a stranger and you welcomed me'. The Benedictine rule indeed roots itself in scripture, the practice of 'holy reading' (Lectio Divina) being originally a Benedictine practice. The importance of prayerfully being soaked in the Bible and resting in silence to hear God's word is a distinctively Benedictine practice. Father Cyprian Smith, from the Benedictine Monastery at Appleforth, comments on this important aspect of Benedict's teaching:

> We are reminded that The Rule of St Benedict begins with the word, "listen". Properly understood, this is the key to his whole teaching. A monk should be above all a listener. So indeed should every Christian. The whole spiritual life of a Christian is a process of listening to God, inclining the ear of the heart. This image of the inward ear, the ear of the heart, shows us that our listening is not merely an intellectual or rational activity, it is intuitive, springing from the very core of our being; where we are most open to God, most receptive to the word he speaks.[132]

As with Augustine the rule requires three fundamental vows. Yet here, too, Benedict shows his humanity; for him, these are virtues to which members of his community are called to return over and over again. They are not the harsh detachment from the ordinary affections and life of the world. Rather, the rule of

---

[132] *The Path of Life* by Cyprian Smith, OSB, Gracewing, 1996, pp.6–7.

Benedict is based on three principles, which at their heart are not world denying but rather for the building up of the individual's relationship with God. Obedience is the first; this vow is about the fundamental relationship with God. Benedict understands God to be love; therefore, it is an obedience to be loved. In this understanding, Benedict echoes Antony's teaching to follow Christ's commandment from John's gospel: to be obedient to love. Obedience is not therefore to be understood to be adhering to the authority of the abbot. Rather, it is the gift of the free will to ascend into the love of the Father. It is also obedience to the community to recognise that those who are also loved by God are our brothers and sisters. De Waal recognises this as being fundamental to the rule:

> It is the new understanding of the relationships between the members of the community that is the great breakthrough. The older ideal had been essentially that of a novice finding a holy man and asking to learn from him, and the monastery had been a group of individuals gathered round the feet of a sage. One of these earlier rules, "The Rule of the Master" had given enormous power to the abbot. St Benedict changes this almost exclusively vertical pattern of authority by emphasizing the relationships of the monks with each other. They are of course disciples who have come to the monastery to be trained, but they are also brothers bound in love to each other.[133]

Second is the vow of stability. Benedictines, unlike other religious orders, join a community rather than the order itself. This means there is commitment to be in a loving fellowship with one another. In 2012, I attended Vespers at Ampleforth; the

---

[133] De Waal op. cit. p.4.

abbot explained that this was the one office that continued in Latin when the others had been changed to English. What was the reason for this? 'In order', explained the abbot, 'that the departed brothers could still join in with the present community in prayer'. That could only happen in a Benedictine house. This vow of stability demonstrates a realistic understanding that the way of a Christian can be hard. Difficulties are not to be avoided; rather, they are to be faced, worked through and overcome. It is important to note that Benedict gives a great deal of teaching on this subject. His 'twelve steps of humility' describe an inwards conversion of the heart that leads to a change in our outwards behaviour. His teaching is as ever rooted in scripture, in the example of Jesus from the gospels. He advises that as we get closer to Christ in our relationship of prayer, the greater the divine presence, the more dignity is given to our littleness.

Third, there is the vow which is difficult to translate into English. 'Conversatio morum' is a Latin expression which means 'conversation of life' but is perhaps better translated as 'faithfully living'. This is much more than chastity and poverty. For unlike many other rules and especially Augustine's, this is not detachment from the world but rather embracing life. It is about being open to the world but remaining faithful, being willing to follow where Christ leads. 'We believe that the divine presence is everywhere', comments St Benedict. 'We should believe this all the more, without any doubt whatsoever, when we attend to the divine work'.[134]

Thus, Benedictine houses are places of prayer. The context, though, of prayer was different from that of their Augustinian

---

[134] Ibid., p.55.

brothers and sisters. For Benedict, prayer was the aim of the rule, which is why most of his teaching on the subject comes as a summary of all that has gone before. Prayer is the culmination, the fulfilment of the rule; his communities are called to live prayerfully. De Waal sums this up well:

> Prayer lies at the very heart of the Benedictine life; it holds everything together, it sustains every other activity. It is at the same time root and fruit, foundation and fulfilment. Prayer is the one thing that makes all the rest possible. For praying can never be set apart from the rest of life, it is the life itself. St Benedict did not ask his monks to take a vow to pray, for he expected prayer to be central in their lives, permeating whatever else they were doing. Prayer is opus dei, the work of God, and nothing whatsoever is to be preferred to it. At least twice St Benedict says nothing must be put before the love of Christ, and he uses precisely the same phrase "to put nothing before" when he comes to talk of the divine office, as if that is the most excellent witness to the community's love of Christ, the pre-eminent occasion for the expression of that love.[135]

For modern contemplatives, therefore, the Benedictine rule is summed up in his phrase 'Conversatio morum', which is of greatest importance. The conversion of life neatly encapsulates the teaching of some contemporary Benedictines through the WCCM. Meditation is specific to Benedict and his understanding of contemplative prayer. 'Meditatio' literally means 'to chew over', and Benedict, in encouraging his order to be 'soaked in scripture', he advises in the practice of Lectio Divina a method of 'chewing over' a particular text. In the last

---

[135] Ibid., p.129.

fifty years, though, the Benedictine contemplative way has become increasingly popular, and the WCCM has grown far beyond the traditional reach of the order. John Main is the key catalyst of this movement; Laurence Freeman, the current leader of the movement, tells of its beginnings:

> In 1954 John Main, as a practicing Roman Catholic, was taught meditation by a holy Indian teacher in Malaya. He was taught to repeat a single (Christian) phrase for the time of his meditation. He continued to worship and study in the Church and eventually was led to become a monk. One day during a crucial time in his life he read John Cassian and because of his previous experience of meditation, was able to recognise Cassian's meditation as substantially identical with what he had learned from his Indian teacher. He had been led back onto his own personal spiritual pilgrimage.[136]

John Main discovered in his own life as a Benedictine the teaching of Antony, which transformed him, enabling him to make sense of his previous spiritual encounter. Like Antony, he came to understand the primacy of silence for the contemplative life. Main himself reflects on this transformation in his own life:

> Meditation is not the time for words, however beautiful and sincerely phrased. All our words are wholly ineffective when we come to enter into this deep and mysterious communion with God. In a deep creative silence we meet God in a way that transcends all our powers of intellect and language. We

---

[136] *Light Within* by Laurence Freeman, OSB, Canterbury Press, Norwich, 1986, p.5.

know that God is intimately with us and we know also that He is infinitely beyond us.[137]

It is the form of silent prayer through which Main understands the Christian to be in relationship with God by the power of the Spirit and focused on the person of Jesus. He tells us how we enter into this relationship each day:

> The qualities we need in this fundamental encounter between ourselves and the ground of our being are attentiveness and receptivity. In order to realise our complete incorporation with the Word, we have not only to listen to its silence, the silence within us, but also to allow the cycle of its life to be completed in us and to lead us into the depth of its silence. There in the silence of the Word we share His experience of hearing the word spoken by the Father.[138]

John Main reminds us that prayer is about our relationship with God, the divine within us; it is about the formation of our discipleship, our journey of faith and the nourishment of our souls. In this, his teaching is rooted in that of the desert fathers and mothers and their belief in the prayer of the heart. This transformation of life is a vocation for contemplatives. Paul Harris, a founding member of WCCM with John Main and Laurence Freeman, sees this transformation as key; 'What we do in meditation is to go beyond words and thought to rest in the Lord and to allow God to pray within us'.[139] This understanding of silent prayer leading the contemplative to 'rest' is the same as

---

[137] Main op. cit. p.7.

[138] John Main, *Word into Silence,* Paulist Press, 1981, p.34.

[139] *Christian Meditation* by Paul Harris, DLT, London, 1996, p.3.

the teaching of the desert fathers and mothers. The primacy of silence for the loving relationship with the divine within is central to the modern Benedictine concept of 'conversion of life'. Harris writes of John Main himself:

> John Main reminds us that meditation is not primarily a way of doing but is a way of becoming, becoming ourselves and coming to self-knowledge. He says that in this way of prayer we seek to become the person we are called to be, that meditation is not about doing but about being.[140]

In a similar way, Sarah Bachelard, a contemporary WCCM member who has established a contemplative network in Australia, sees this path in vocational terms. The transformation of the divine relationship is a recognition 'of the truth that God is the God who addresses us. The call of God is often to a life more dangerous, uncertain and frightening than the lives we attempt to secure for ourselves'.[141] The transformation that comes as a result of resting in this challenging relationship of love can be unsettling, but it is life-changing and takes us to a new place which she describes as 'unselfing':

> Here it is not that we are consciously unselfish, or nobly self-forgetful; it is simply that we no longer have an ego capable of propping itself up or seeking to keep itself separate. Once I realised not only that I could not remake myself but that mercifully I did not have to, I entered the realm of grace. I entered the place where I could receive as

---

[140] Ibid., p.3.
[141] *Experiencing God in a Time of Crisis* by Sarah Bachelard, Meditatio, London, 2017, p.17.

gift that which I had striven all my life, a sense of being at home with myself, with others and with reality.[142]

This sense of transformation leading to personal freedom is close to the liberation felt by Antony and those who lived in retreat in the desert.

Benedictine meditation is based on this transforming relationship of the divine within by the grace of God in the loving heart of Jesus. Main came to understand this as clearly as Antony and any of the great desert teachers had; he writes:

> In its essential significance, the aim of meditation is just this: the realisation of our total incorporation in Jesus Christ, in the cycle of his utterance by, and return to, the Father. The qualities we need in this fundamental encounter between ourselves and the ground of our being are attentiveness and receptivity. In order to realise our complete incorporation with the Word, we have not only to listen to its silence, the silence within us, but to allow the cycle of its life to be completed in us and to lead us into the depth of its silence. There in the silence of the Word we share His experience of hearing Himself eternally spoken by the Father.[143]

The way of contemplation is therefore a way of incorporation into the eternal abiding of Jesus and his Father as described in John's gospel and explored by Antony.

For contemporary Benedictines, both as part of the order and as part of the wider school of contemplation in WCCM, meditation

---

[142] Ibid., p.46.
[143] Main op. cit., p.34.

leads us into the fullness of life promised by Jesus, lived in the desert by Antony. John Main sums up for us what this means:

> In meditating we do affirm our faith in the gift of our own creation. We recognise the wonder of our own being. Jesus has told us that His mission was to bring us fullness of life. In making this declaration, He assures in the same gospel of St John, that it is He Himself who is the Way to this fullness. He tells us that He is the Light of the world and, no follower of mine shall wander in the dark; he shall have the light of life. In beginning to meditate we are declaring a courageous acceptance of this invitation of Jesus and we enter into our meditation on each occasion as the twin process of vitalization and enlightenment.[144]

---

[144] Ibid., p.19.

Chapter Nine: Becoming Silence

Prayer is sitting in the silence until it silences us, choosing gratitude until we are grateful, and praising God until we ourselves are an act of praise.[145] *– Richard Rohr*

Francis of Assisi was as much of an anarchist as any of the abbas or ammas of the fourth century. Like Antony before him, he was outraged by the greed and power of the church in his own day. It was a time of enormous change. In the previous century, the Papal States had been formed, the Pope becoming both a spiritual leader and warlord in Europe. At the same time, successive popes had adopted the title 'vicar of Christ'; prior to the eleventh century, the Bishop of Rome had been known as the 'vicar of St Peter's tomb'. The difference between the two titles is of course enormous and represents a spiritual power grab. Francis himself came from a very wealthy family and, after being taken prisoner, came to renounce his old life and rather committed himself to serve the poor. Like Antony, he retreated from the city, at first living in a cave. His example of caring for the poor encouraged his followers to copy his simple pattern of life caring for the needy. He encouraged his followers, 'While you are proclaiming peace with your lips, be careful to have it even more fully in your heart'.[146] Francis followed the life of a contemplative and chose to pray in quiet and lonely places. He counted himself as a mystic, having several visions of Christ which directed and changed his life. His last vision was on 14 September 1224 and, after he returned to his cell, lived a life of silent prayer, encouraging others, saying, 'We

---

[145] *Falling Upwards* by Richard Rohr, SPCK, London, 2012.
[146] *St Francis of Assisi* by Jon Sweeney, Griffin, 2019, p.45.

should seek not so much to pray but to become prayer',[147] before dying on 3 October 1226. Francis transformed the European church and brought contemplative practice and mysticism back into the central life of Western thought and belief.

Francis is well-known for his love of creation and animals. His love of God's world, though, was rooted in his understanding of the relationship between the creation and the Creator. His most famous prayer, 'The Canticle of the Sun', extols this relationship:

> Be praised, my Lord, through all your creatures, especially through my lord Brother Sun, who brings the day; and you give light through him. And he is beautiful and radiant in all his splendour! Of you, Most High, he bears the likeness.
> Be praised, my Lord, through Sister Moon and the stars; in the heavens you have made them, precious and beautiful.
> Be praised, my Lord, through Brothers Wind and Air, and clouds and storms, and all the weather, through which you give your creatures sustenance.
> Be praised, My Lord, through Sister Water; she is very useful, and humble, and precious, and pure.
> Be praised, my Lord, through Brother Fire, through whom you brighten the night. He is beautiful and cheerful, and powerful and strong.
> Be praised, my Lord, through our sister Mother Earth, who feeds us and rules us, and produces various fruits with coloured flowers and herbs.
> Be praised, my Lord, through those who forgive for love of

---

[147] Ibid., p.72.

you; through those who endure sickness and trial. Happy those who endure in peace, for they will be crowned.[148]

Francis echoes Antony and Augustine in understanding the sacred nature of being God's creation and how he is known through the silence of the land. Like the saints of Celtic spirituality, he perceived Christ in relationship with the world. His visions of Christ often took place in the wildest and remotest places.

The late medieval centuries saw a revival in mysticism. Mysticism whilst sometimes being related to visions is best understood as being part of the contemplative tradition, in that the mystic seeks union with the divine which may be attained by self-surrender. Contemplatives can sometimes experience visions of Christ or Mary, which proved to be transformative. The anonymous author of 'The Cloud of Unknowing' draws on the mystical tradition of Christian Neoplatonism, which focuses on discovering God as the source of everything, beyond mental conception and thus without any definitive image or form:

> For I tell you this: one loving, blind desire for God alone is more valuable in itself, more pleasing to God and to the saints, more beneficial to your own growth, and more helpful to your friends, both living and dead, than anything else you could do.[149]

Most famous of these fourteenth-century English mystics is the anchorite who had her cell at St Julian's Church in Norwich.

---

[148] Ibid., p.83.
[149] *The Cloud of Unknowing,* edited by Evelyn Underhill, St Anthanasius Press, 2017, p.55.

Her account of her visions of the love of Christ echoes the teachings of the desert mothers:

> I saw that it is indeed more worthy of God and more truly pleasing to him that through his goodness we should pray with full confidence, and by his grace cling to him with real understanding and unshakeable love, than that we should go on making as many petitions as our souls are capable of.[150]

Like Antony and Francis, she also identified the love of God as being revealed through creation as well as scripture:

> In this he showed me a little thing, the quantity of a hazel nut, lying in the palm of my hand, as it seemed. And it was as round as any ball. I looked upon it with the eye of my understanding, and thought, "What may this be?" And it was answered generally thus, "It is all that is made". I marvelled how it might last, for I thought it might suddenly have fallen to nothing for littleness. And I was answered in my understanding: It lasts and ever shall, for God loves it. And so have all things their beginning by the love of God.[151]

The simplicity of her writing conveys the power of her visions and her experience of God's love, concluding in the clearest of spiritual formulas: 'In this little thing I saw three properties. The first is that God made it. The second that God loves it. And the third, that God keeps it'.[152] The third of these fourteenth-century mystics is Walter Hilton, but his writings have been less well-

---

[150] *Revelations of Divine Love,* translated by Barry Windeatt, OUP, Oxford, 2015, p.91.
[151] Ibid., p.153.
[152] Ibid., p.154.

known. Like many of the desert teachers, he speaks of the experience of contemplation being rooted in humility:

> One who loves God retains this humility at all times, not with weariness and struggle, but with pleasure and gladness … What is humility but truthfulness? There is no real difference.[153]

The contemplative revival, linked with the mysticism of the thirteenth and fourteenth centuries, was part of the events which gave rise to the split in the Western Church, which we refer to as the Reformation. Eamon Duffy has shown that far from being spiritually dead, the church in the lives of ordinary Christians was vibrant and deeply rooted. The popularity of mystical writers suggests the contemplative life was widely practised.

Whilst Christianity itself became a battleground in the sixteenth century, this rootedness of contemplation found new voices in the writings of the renewed Carmelite order. Teresa of Avila was charismatic in the sixteenth century in Europe as Francis was three centuries earlier. 'Prayer is an act of love', advised Teresa. 'Words are not needed'.[154] This is a familiar sentiment in the teaching of Antony and Augustine of Hippo. It is Teresa herself who gives us an image from the natural world of the silk worm spinning its own cocoon from which it eventually emerges transformed to be a parable of the transformation of the contemplative life. She concludes:

---

[153] *Walter Hilton Collection* by Walter Hilton, Aeterna Press, New York, 2016, p.34.
[154] Interior Castle op. cit. p.22.

How much, by God's grace, we can do, by preparing this home [the cocoon] for ourselves, towards making Him our dwelling-place as He is in the prayer of union. You will suppose that I mean we can take away from or add something to God when I say that He is our home, and that we can make this home and dwell in it by our own power. Indeed we can: though we can neither deprive God of anything nor add aught to Him, yet we can take away from and add to ourselves, like the silkworms. The little we can do will hardly have been accomplished when this insignificant work of ours, which amounts to nothing at all, will be united by God to His greatness and thus enhanced with such immense value that our Lord Himself will be the reward of our toil.[155]

Both Teresa of Avila and John of the Cross from the sixteenth-century Carmelites still speak to the modern contemplative, but perhaps the greatest influence from this time is Ignatius of Loyola. The importance of Ignatian spirituality for modern contemplatives should not be overlooked. The spiritual exercises are used by many Christians, most of whom are not Roman Catholics. The prayer of Examen is used by those training to be spiritual directors, and many people use the practice of gospel contemplation without realising its origin. Ignatius was born in 1491 in Spain, one of thirteen children, and as with many of the sons of the aristocracy, he became a knight. Seriously injured in 1521, he had a series of spiritual awakenings over the months of his convalescence. His attention focused on the life of Jesus and of saints, who cheered him during his painful recovery. Ignatius believed in the importance of education and disciplined study to effect change. Having made a pilgrimage to Jerusalem, he

---

[155] Ibid., p.47.

returned home and studied for two years in Barcelona. Even by this time he had attracted followers, and so the spiritual exercises were written for this embryonic fellowship.

The spiritual exercises were conceived by Ignatius to be threefold. There is the relationship between the spiritual director and exercitant (the person who follows the exercises), the exercitant and God, and God and the spiritual director. In this way, the prayer is always guided, and the practice of prayer is very similar to the desert tradition of seeking advice from a more experienced pupil of prayer, their abba or amma. The full set of exercises takes place over thirty days, and therefore, these are rarely completed more than once or twice in a lifetime. The impact of this guided prayer can be transformative. Yet the various elements of the exercises can be used by anyone in their daily lives. The ways of praying first used by Ignatius and his followers resonate in the modern contemplative mind. His almost conversational style is so helpful to those put off by the formality of Christian worship. They concentrate on the person of Jesus, which is refreshing simple amid all the 'doctrines' of the church. Jim Manney sums up this attractive spiritual teaching commenting on the widespread use of the most popular exercise:

> The Examen isn't the only way to pray but it's a way that everyone can pray. It banishes the abstract and relishes the concrete. It is inexhaustible. It treats every moment of everyday as a blessed time when God can appear. It's a way to find God in all things.[156]

---

[156] *A Simple Life-changing Prayer* by Jim Manney, Loyola Press, Chicago, 2011, p.4.

Mysticism, as part of the contemplative life, is fundamental, and the nineteenth- and twentieth-century revival in silent prayer harked back to the desert teaching. The Oxford Movement popularised reading of the sayings of the desert fathers and mothers. However, it was Evelyn Underhill's book *Mysticism* which served to place the contemplative life into the mainstream of the English churches again, unifying Reformed and Catholic Church styles to see the importance of Antony and the contemplative tradition. She wrote:

> In mysticism that love of truth which we saw as the beginning of all philosophy leaves the merely intellectual sphere, and takes on the assured aspect of a personal passion. Where the philosopher guesses and argues, the mystic lives and looks; and speaks, consequently, the disconcerting language of first-hand experience, not the neat dialectic of the schools. Hence whilst the Absolute of the metaphysicians remains a diagram –impersonal and unattainable – the Absolute of the mystics is lovable, attainable, alive.[157]

Underhill not only helped reshape the liturgy of the churches but also the practice of prayer in embracing the apophatic once more:

> The spiritual life of individuals has to be extended both vertically to God and horizontally to other souls; and the more it grows in both directions, the less merely individual and therefore more truly personal it will become.[158]

---

[157] Evelyn Underhill op. cit. p.92.
[158] Ibid., p.97.

Underhill developed our mainstream churches' understanding of the contemplative life, and as a result, mysticism has a place among current contemplative writers. Maggie Ross is one such writer, who argues for experience and passion over skills and technique. She advises:

> The work of silence is empirical because the mind's progression into silence, and the realisation of the gifts it receives from silence, can be and have been described consistently for millennia across cultures by those who have cared to observe their own minds. Learning to use this rich heritage from the past involves recognising there is nothing 'bad' about the self-conscious mind: it is vital to critical thinking and to stimulating the activities and expanding the scope of the deep mind.[159]

Therefore, the creative use of imagination embraced by the mystic and firmly rooted in the spirituality of Francis, Julian, Teresa and Ignatius speak very clearly to the modern contemplative. For Ross, the experience of silent prayer is mystical in that it transforms us in a way that cannot be analysed or explained. She reflects:

> For millennia, people who have engaged silence have discovered that if self-consciousness appears to be what makes us "homo sapiens" then its elision opens the door to what was once called divinity. If we can move beyond our noisy, circular, manipulative thinking to wait in silence, in attentive receptivity, we open ourselves to insight and to what may appear like behavioural change, but is in fact a

---

[159] *Silence: A User's Guide* by Maggie Ross, DLT, 2014, p.29.

stripping off of dross that masked the unfolding truth of the self in the deep mind, in the heart.[160]

Francis of Assisi was a mystic, but he was also a radical. His radical influence upon the modern contemplative is seen in the writing of Brother Ramon, who often appears to be ahead of contemporary teachings on creation and contemplation by being rooted not just in Franciscan teaching but also in that of the desert fathers and mothers. He comments on their influence, saying:

> The main thrust of what they are saying is that we need to see that innocence, righteousness and love are basic to creation – paradise came before the fall. Therefore, we are made for love, and in spite of the dreadful and universal reality of our fallenness and need for redemption, God's presence and mercy can be traced in creation and in human nature.[161]

Richard Rohr, also a Franciscan, shows this same radicalism and approaches the contemplative life from a perspective of the desert teachings, which challenges and often provokes modern Christians. In his book on the nature of the Trinity, Rohr evokes the mystical spirit of Francis and the obedience to love as taught by Antony. He writes of becoming aware of the flow of love as being the reality of the Trinity for the contemplative. He concludes:

---

[160] Ibid., p.57.

[161] *Heaven on Earth* by Brother Ramon, Marshall Pickering, London, 1991, p.167.

Our final goal of union with God is grounded in creation itself and in our own unique creation. This was the central belief in my own spiritual foundation as a Franciscan friar. Our starting place was always original goodness. This makes our ending place, and everything in between, possessing an inherent capacity for goodness, truth and beauty.[162]

Just as Antony saw the relationship between God and Jesus in terms of 'abiding' in love and the same relationship through the Spirit of 'abiding' in us; in the same way, Rohr understands the primary divine relationship being the flow of love.

In their practice, the desert abbas and ammas placed the greatest emphasis on practical hospitality. So, too, Rohr understands the vocation of the contemplative life is found in divine hospitality. Like them, he uses the image of a resting God when he reflects on this truth:

> It's something you can experience only by resting inside of the relationship of prayer, as when the disciples asked Jesus where he lived, and he offered this intimate invite, "come and see". Divine hospitality at work.[163]

For Rohr, therefore, as for Antony, being obedient to love is to dance in the flow of the Trinity. He understands the immediacy of the present moment in living life to the full, summing up the experience of the contemplative being held in the Trinitarian love, saying:

---

[162] *The Divine Dance* by Richard Rohr, SPCK, London, 2016, p.32.
[163] Ibid., p.91.

We can't diminish God's love for us. What we can do, however, is learn how to believe it, receive it, trust it, allow it, and celebrate it, accepting Trinity's whirling invitation to join in the cosmic dance. That's why all spirituality comes down to how you're doing life right now. How you're doing right now is a microcosm of the whole of your life. How you do anything is how you do everything.[164]

The conclusion of Rohr's radicalism is to bring us to the truth of not only the contemplative life but also to bring alive for our current generation Antony's teaching of loving prayer, loving heart and loving life. Therefore, in summing up for us the transforming impact of apophatic prayer, Rohr declares:

God tries to first create a joyous yes inside you, far more than any kind of no. Then you have become God's full work of art, and for you love is now stronger than death, and Christ is surely risen in you! Love and life have become the same thing.[165]

---

[164] Ibid., p.193.

[165] *Immortal Diamond: The Search for Our True Self* by Richard Rohr, SPCK, 2013, p.182.

Chapter Ten: Doing the Just Thing

Our being Christians today will be limited to two things: praying and doing the just thing.[166] *– Dietrich Bonhoeffer*

Just as Antony in the fourth century was faced by an enormous challenge to faith, Dietrich Bonhoeffer in the 1930s faced the most extreme challenge to truth and living a prayerful life. Ironically, though, despite the violence and cruelty of those times, without doubt the most exciting developments in the Christian faith in the last hundred years around the world can be traced back to the influence of Bonhoeffer. He was born in Breslau, Germany, on 4 February 1906. Dietrich was the son of a university professor and highly educated mother. He was one of eight children, having a twin sister, three other sisters and three brothers. He was brought up as a Christian in a very liberal, humanitarian tradition. His father was a pioneer in psychiatry. He studied at Tubingen and Berlin Universities and was influenced by Karl Barth studying at the Union Theological College in New York. In 1930, he became a lecturer in theology in Berlin.

After Hitler came to power in Germany in 1933, Bonhoeffer was expelled from Berlin University because of his outspoken views. Three years later, he established with Karl Barth and others the Confessing Church. He denounced on the radio the government as corrupt, Hitler as misleading the nation and the churches for co-opting Nazi values. Leaving Germany to pastor a church in London, he got to know George Bell, who became a friend and a

---

[166] *Letters and Papers from Prison*, New York, Macmillian, 1972, p.294.

channel for the views of German opposition. He returned to Germany to found a series of illegal training colleges based on a community model. He was arrested in April 1943. One of his most important works was from this time, *Letters and Papers from Prison*. He was executed at Flossenburg two days before it was liberated by the Allies.

It is in Bonhoeffer's writings as well as the story of his life that we are challenged by his compelling vision that for prayer to be real, it must give rise to action; 'be doers of the word and not merely hearers'.[167] He lived in extraordinary times, and his story, together with his writings, provides a compelling, controversial and challenging witness.

Bonhoeffer's example and influence encouraged others to found nondenominational communities. The key marks were contemplative prayer, communal living at peace with creation, focused on hospitality, engaged in issues of justice and working for reconciliation. George MacLeod was one of those influenced by Bonhoeffer, having met him in London. MacLeod founded the Iona community in 1938; he himself had been profoundly affected by his experience of war. He served at Ypres and Passchendaele, experiencing first-hand the effects of mustard gas. He was awarded the Military Cross for bravery. His experiences led him to train for the ministry. He studied divinity in Edinburgh and New York; upon returning to Scotland, he was invited to become an assistant at St Giles Cathedral. During this period, his concern over social inequality began to become increasingly prominent. In 1924, he was ordained as a minister and became Padre of Toc H (Talbot House) in Scotland. Increasingly, though, he sought a community to express the

---

[167]James 1:22.

compassion and challenge he found in the life of Columcille and in his understanding of the gospel. He obtained permission to live at Iona with a small group, and together they founded the Iona community. He came also to have a prophetic voice on the need to have an environmental conscience in relation to the stewardship of creation.

Roger Schutz graduated in 1939 in Switzerland. The communities that Bonhoeffer had created for the Confessing Church influenced him. Schutz and his fellow students met daily for prayer and Bible study. It was the fall of France in May 1940 that convinced him and his friends to travel to the Vichy area to found a house of prayer to assist those most discouraged and in despair. The farm at Taizé was bought from the sale of the first community members' cars. A simple rule was established, and by the end of 1945, the community had seven brothers. During the war, the community worked to protect the local people from the Gestapo, being a refuge for those escaping from the Nazis including many hundreds of Jews. From 1945, Taizé was renamed the 'Community of Reconciliation'. For Brother Roger, the idea of a contemplative community was rooted in the idea of sacred unity:

> What I was passionately seeking, I believe, is something very concrete', he reflected later in life, 'a parable of communion incarnate in the lives of a few people, for words have no credibility until they are lived out. I was haunted by the idea: why not put into the dough of the divided churches, indeed all the churches, a leaven of communion?[168]

---

[168] *Taize* by Rex Brico, Collins, London, 1978, p.181.

The violent destruction and chaos of the Second World War proved to be a catalyst for Christians finding new meaning in the old teaching of the desert fathers and mothers. Bonhoeffer was the touchstone for all this, but he wasn't alone. Chiara Lubich, in her homeland of Italy, found also new meaning in silent prayer with a small group of followers amid the ruins of her society. Her burning desire to live in peace and unity has driven the Focolare movement ever since; in a visit to the United Nations in 2000, she commented, 'Our love serves to bring different people together in unity. This will bring to life a new world renewed by love, where everyone will feel as brothers and sisters of the one God'.[169]

There is also an echo of the desert teaching of the loving heart which alone brings freedom in the reflections of Pope John Paul II of his experience of living under the persecution of first the Nazis and then the Communists. At the end of his life, he reflected:

> The greatest light comes from the commandment to love God and neighbour. In this commandment, human freedom finds its most complete realisation. Freedom is for love: its realisation through love can reach heroic proportions. Christ speaks of laying down his life for his friends, for other human beings. In the history of Christianity, many people in different ways have laid down their lives for their neighbour, and they have done so in order to follow the example of Christ.[170]

---

[169] *Chiara Lubich: A Biography* by Armando Torno, New City Press, New York, 2012.
[170] *Memory and Identity* by John Paul II, Weidenfeld & Nicolson, London, 2005.

Part of the openness to the contemplative life was to be found in a willingness to look back into the history of Christianity to find examples of those who have faced crises in the past and found meaning in the desert teaching. When asked about his inspiration, Brother Roger commented in 1978:

> Among the witnesses to Christ I esteem Teresa of Avila most of all because of the fire within her, the way she totally gave her life, while at the same time retaining her realism and her ability to achieve concrete results. She combined the two dimensions, the practical and the spiritual, within herself.[171]

Perhaps it was the combination of Bonhoeffer's practical and spiritual approaches that was so influential. His foresight about the crisis facing the church in the wake of the great suffering of war and the need for a new beginning touched the hearts of many. Undoubtedly his death marked him out as a Christian martyr who had laid down his life not just in opposition to a monstrous evil but also for a new way of embracing the loving heart of Jesus. Key to Bonhoeffer's teaching was the link between 'prayer and action'. When Bonhoeffer returned from the USA in 1939, he said:

> I shall have no right to participate in the reconstruction of Christian life in Germany after the war if I do not share the trials of this time with my people. Christians in Germany will face the terrible alternative of either willing the defeat of their nation in order that Christian civilization may survive, or willing the victory of their nation and thereby

---

[171] Brico op. cit. p.192.

destroying civilization. I know which of those alternatives I must choose; but I cannot make this choice in security.[172]

After his arrest, Bonhoeffer wrote from prison, 'Our being Christians today will be limited to two things: praying and doing the just thing'.[173] Restricted though he was in prison, he sought to live out his advice to others; as well as following a daily programme of prayer and silent contemplation, he also sought to do 'the just thing'. As a prisoner, he organised legal advice, money for fellow prisoners' families, arranged air-raid procedure, acted as a medical assistant and refused to move to a more comfortable imprisonment to continue supporting others in the Gestapo prison at Tegel.

Bonhoeffer believed that there was a necessary balance between prayer and action. He identified four key issues:
- doing 'the just thing' keeps prayer from escaping into self-sufficient piety, and praying keeps doing 'the just thing' from self-righteousness;
- doing 'the just thing' keeps praying from hypocrisy, and praying keeps 'the just thing' from fanaticised ideology;
- doing 'the just thing' keeps praying from pessimism, and praying keeps 'the just thing' from resignation;
- doing 'the just thing' keeps praying grounded in reality, and praying keeps doing 'the just thing' rooted in gospel values.[174]

---

[172] Eric Metaxes, *Bonheoffer*, Thomas Nelson, 2011, p.422.
[173] *Letters and Papers from Prison*, New York, Macmillian, 1972, p.294
[174] *The Cost of Discipleship*, SCM, 1964, p.46.

In the 1950s, both Taizé and Iona grew and flourished, becoming increasingly influential. Pope John XXIII referred to Taizé as 'the springtime of the church'. Taizé became the first multidenominational community to include Roman Catholics. Iona inspired other communities and developed an international network of 'family groups' in which thousands followed a simple rule. The Northumbrian community, Corrymeela and other Celtic communities are all rooted in the original Iona community, but each has different areas of spiritual work.

The idea of communities of prayer has also flourished in new ways. Bede Griffiths stayed at a Hindu ashram in the 1960s and, from 1968, founded his Christian ashram based on contemplative prayer and reconciliation between those of different faiths. His writings have been very important in developing creation spirituality and mysticism of New Monasticism. Bede, together with the Benedictine John Main, popularised Christian meditation. John Main founded the WCCM with Laurence Freeman in 1975 at Ealing Abbey.

In the USA, Bonhoeffer's example inspired the 'Simple Way' which began in Philadelphia in the 1970s. Jonathan Wilson, in his 1998 book *Living Faithfully in a Fragmented World,* first suggested the term 'new monasticism'. Wilson pointed to the foundation of Bonhoeffer and quoted him as saying, 'The restoration of the church will surely come from a new type of monasticism which has nothing in common with the old but a complete lack of compromise in a life lived in accordance with the Sermon on the Mount in the discipleship of Christ'.[175]
Wilson's daughter, Leah Wilson-Hartgrove, is one of the founders of Rutba House in 2004 in North Carolina, which has

---

[175] Metaxes op. cit. p.512.

devised the twelve principles of New Monasticism, which is known as the 'Simple Way'. This movement in the United States has also inspired contemplative groups such as the 'Abbey of the Arts', who have directly looked back to the desert teaching and rooted themselves in an environmental theology of creation. Christine Paintner, in her influential book *The Soul of the Pilgrim,* evokes much of the language of *The Philokalia.* She says of contemplation:

> In your imagination, see yourself at a doorway. Spend some time being with the door and noticing its qualities. What are the colours and textures? Is it old or new? Is it worn with time or shiny? Is it closed or slightly ajar? See if you can be with whatever image comes to mind without trying to change it. Imagine yourself pausing here, knowing that as you cross this threshold you enter into a liminal kind of time, Kairos as the ancient teachers called it. This is time outside time, where you will encounter both challenge and grace.[176]

Paintner calls this way of contemplation 'the soulful journey', and she links this to the understanding of faith from the desert tradition:

> The soulful journey goes straight through the heart of the desert. In the middle of that parched land, where everything comfortable is stripped away, we often find ourselves wanting to run or go to sleep. Monastic spirituality calls us to return to the practice of showing up, of being still, of opening our hearts to an encounter with the holy. In the sayings of the desert fathers we hear this story full of

---

[176] *The Soul of a Pilgrim* by Christine Paintner, Ave Marie Press, 2015, p.6.

wisdom, "Abba Moses asked Abba Silvanus, 'Can a man lay a new foundation every day?'. The old man replied, 'If he works hard he can lay a new foundation at every moment'. And also this story, Abba Poemen said about Abba Pior that every single day he made a fresh beginning".[177]

Paintner expresses that rediscovery for new generations of the wisdom of the desert teaching is at the heart of the new monastic communities.

New Monasticism is growing across the world and is one of the most dynamic forms of growth in modern Christianity. Often the communities sit alongside traditional denominations and are more attractive to those who are alienated by formal 'stuffy' church life. Communities are not limited to one style of churchmanship or denomination. Often the communities overlap traditional boundaries in new and exciting ways.

Bonhoeffer's legacy is profound for the modern church. His life and writings still make uncomfortable reading and challenge today's churches. Who knows what the modern church would have come to look like under his personal influence? In many ways, the community at Taizé, the struggle of Eastern European churches, as well as the South African church and the liberation churches of South America all represent his legacy. In the words of his godson Eberhard Bethage, 'He has become an inextinguishable sign of hope for oppressed people far beyond the borders of his own county'.[178]

---

[177] Ibid., p.98.

[178] Eberhard Bethage, *Prayer and Righteous Action*, Christian Journals, Belfast, 1979, p.45.

These last five chapters have sought to show that so much of our contemporary teaching about contemplative prayer has a great deal in common with Antony and his example. It is striking that so often silent prayer has a central place in these renewal communities in the church. The apophatic prayer taught by the desert fathers and mothers has found again a new resonance in the lives of people around the world. Who knows the reasons for this? Certainly, it is the work of the Holy Spirit. Perhaps also it is a reaction to the old certainties being destroyed by the world at war, the hatreds that were fostered and the current divisions and inequalities of humanity. Perhaps, too, a new consciousness of fragility of our plant and the unstainable nature of our lifestyles are causing us to return to a spiritual home amid the pressures we face.

In this book, I have traced the contemplative tradition as it has come down to us in Britain. I have explored the teaching and example of Antony and the earliest desert fathers and mothers, summing this example up in five themes: being obedient to love; loving prayer; loving community; loving heart and loving life. Following on from this, I have attempted to demonstrate how contemporary contemplative writers have drawn upon the desert teaching both directly and indirectly and how the great spiritualities of the church are themselves rooted in the desert. Moving into the last section of this book, I will now attempt to answer my own question, which is the reason for writing this book. How can we follow a contemplative way living a busy modern life? Antony told his followers to be faithful in their practice of silent prayer and that their own soul's desire would teach them. This is a challenge for us. The ability to still our minds and to open ourselves to the divine within is something we all find difficult. We recognise that apophatic prayer can enrich our lives and faith. More than this, though, is the truth that in silence itself, we come to encounter God, who abides in us, and to recognise that we abide in him. John Main sums this up this great truth for us in a simple yet profound concluding statement:

Our language is wholly inadequate and our thought too self-conscious to reflect the simplicity and actuality of God's love. But it is not language or thought we need. We need only to become aware of the mystery within us, the silence in which we see our own soul.[179]

---

[179] Main op. cit. p.35.

Chapter Eleven: The Priority of Silence

Silence is the language of the Spirit.[180] *– John Main*

What does it mean to be a modern contemplative? How can we follow a contemplative path in daily life? Are there key principles that we can all base our lives upon if we call ourselves 'contemplatives'?

The words 'contemplation' and 'meditation' are of course both specifically Christian. Although used more widely in the modern world to cover a whole variety of practices which aim to help individuals become more peaceful and less stressed, these terms have their origins within Christianity. Both contemplation and meditation are from Latin words and have their meanings rooted within the teaching of the desert fathers and mothers and the tradition they established. The first use of 'contemplatio' was in the fourth century; its meaning is literally to 'muse upon the place of the divine dwelling'. Its use was in the context of advice about the indwelling light or spirit within the soul. 'Meditatio' was first used by Benedict in his rule; its literal meaning is 'to chew over', and he used this word in relation to 'spiritual' nourishing in scripture, prayer or silence. Whilst contemplation and meditation now have come to be used more widely, it is worth remembering the way in which these two terms were originally used and their distinctive Christian meanings.

So, if to be a contemplative means to muse upon the indwelling light, the divine in our souls, how do we do this in daily life? All

---

[180] Ibid., p.22.

those mentioned in this book have in some sense been full-time contemplatives. Antony retreated to the desert and lived a contemplative life. The desert fathers and mothers were influenced by Antony and sought to emulate his pattern of life. Augustine of Hippo encouraged his disciples to develop a rule of life, which gave structure to each day to contemplate. Cassian's conferences influenced Martin of Tours, who in turn created the context for first Ninian and then Patrick to develop Irish communities associated with the practice of daily contemplation in creation. Benedict was the first to write a rule, and contemplation was given a structure, which meant that each day was in some sense built around this musing. Meditation was becoming a key element of contemplation. Francis of Assisi was a contemplative and took himself first of all to a cave to retreat from the corruption of the world. Julian of Norwich was walled up into her cell to allow for contemplation to become her sole activity. Teresa of Avila, John of the Cross and Ignatius of Loyola all show a pattern of contemplation, which was the priority of their daily life. In the modern world, Bonhoeffer, of course, was exiled from his homeland, university life and then imprisoned; contemplation was the one consistent in his life. The New Monasticism of the modern world is based on full-time communities; Iona, Corrymeela and Taize all being prime examples. However, over the centuries, there have been many who have 'associated' themselves with these full-time religious contemplatives. Tertiary Franciscans were an early example to offer a structured contemplative without giving up daily life to enter a monastery or convent. In our modern world, though, even the WCCM has after nearly forty years felt it necessary to have a 'religious centre' to maintain the community's contemplative heart.

Is it possible therefore to be a contemplative in daily life? Do we need to give up our worldly occupations to follow a contemplative path? Do we need to become a full-time religious to be called a contemplative? Despite the many examples from this book of just such people who have followed this way or who still do, the answer is no. One of the great encouragements for all of us is that millions who are contemplatives in daily life are often unseen or known only to themselves but define their lives in this way. The teaching of Antony and the early desert teachers was to be faithful to silent prayer above all else. Their advice was simple: that your cell would teach you all you needed to know. At the beginning of this book, I quoted Antony's advice that if you are faithful in prayer, your own 'soul's desire' will teach you all you need to know. The problem therefore is that if you are not a full-time religious, how can you maintain this daily discipline among all the distractions of modern living?

I have been a spiritual director offering spiritual accompaniment for over thirty-five years. During this time, the most frequently raised difficulty by those whom I have sat with is the problem of being 'time poor'. In other words, not being able to make silent prayer the priority. We forget that the word 'priority' is also Latin in origin and means 'of first importance'. In the modern world, we often speak of priorities, but of course, this is nonsense; we cannot have more than one priority. We have to become disciplined and make prayer the priority; like the full-time religious, our rule of life must give structure to our daily life, and we mustn't let our busy life restrict and confine our prayer life. To be a contemplative is to live the whole of our lives in an attitude of contemplation. The mistake often is to think that prayer is an activity something we do when the truth is that prayer is a way of life. Prayer is a relationship with the divine within and without, and only sometimes do we need to use words; most often, we need simply to be aware, and that requires us to be attentive. Often it has been said to me that a person doesn't have time to pray, but the truth is quite the opposite; they are so busy that they need to pray. A way into understanding this is to keep a daily journal for two weeks. Simply at the end of each day, note down what you have done. Even if your life appears to be crazy busy, the demands upon your time unending and there is no space, you will notice that you already do have a daily rhythm. This is what I sometimes do with those I accompany; I get them to become aware of the pattern that already exists and then to make very small changes to place their busy lives into the context of prayer. The impact on those who do this is profound; many people have described this as transformative, like scales falling from their eyes. The simple truth, of course, is that none of us are too busy to be contemplatives; we just think we are or choose to make this excuse.

Contemplation, of course, is not for everyone. It would be foolish to think that there is one path to God which is the same for every person in the world. Contemplation is of course easier for certain personalities, but it doesn't depend upon your psychological profile; rather it is about attitude, desire and longing. Once we recognise, in Laird's words, the inner doorways of our soul, then many of us seek to enter more and more deeply into the inner life, the light within which enlightens the whole of our lives. The first step is to give priority to silence, to make our daily silence as much part of our everyday routine as cleaning our teeth or washing our face. It is helpful if we aren't too precious about how we keep the space to be silent. There isn't one way that works for all. For those who are uncertain, the two-week journal will offer clues as to when and how the space may be found to make silence part of our daily discipline. For one person, it might be to delay turning on their computer and use a short time at their desk before starting work for the day in silent meditation. For a parent, it might be the quiet time after leaving the children at nursery or school before getting on with the next part of the day. For some, they will need a physical prayer space; for others, it is rather the correct attitude to prayer which is key. For some, silence can be found in creation and the outdoors; for others, the pace of walking or running can create the space for silent contemplation. It can take many years to develop your own rule of life which truly reflects your daily rhythm of living and enables you to go deeper into your relationship with God. It may be that a prayer technique may help; for centuries, many Christians have followed the Jesus prayer. The WCCM promoted the use of 'marantha' as a prayer word, and Thomas Keating's centring prayer movement has encouraged followers to find their own 'word'. The technique is only a way to create an approach to being attentive that works for the individual; it isn't the prayer itself. It is important to recognise that silence is the language of the Holy Spirit; the contemplative, in entering into prayer, comes to know the divine within their soul and recognise the primacy of this relationship.

The priority of silence is the vital first principle of being a contemplative. To be silent each day and committed to this practice is the unique feature of the contemplative life. Those who commit themselves to this discipline will seek it each day. If for any reason we are distracted or unable to hold the silence in our usual way, we will be uncomfortable and find it difficult to concentrate on any task. Having said this, there will be times when we find entering into silence almost impossible. We might be very experienced in contemplation, but we all have times when our practice of silent prayer proves very difficult. This has been the experience of contemplatives from the beginning, and it is in these times that we have to become spiritually resilient. When Antony was asked about this, he would ask his questioners the same question: 'What happens each morning in the East?' And after a time, most would understand his question and reply, 'The sun rises'. Antony would then reply, 'And a new day begins'. In the same way, when your prayer seems difficult or too hard, remember that tomorrow is another day, and you can start again. For Antony, silent prayer was the daily priority; its discipline was a channel for the daily desire for contemplation. Even when we achieve it doesn't mean that we will succeed in encountering the divine within; in fact we can all go through extended periods of experiencing nothing in silence and can feel this is all a waste of time. Teresa of Avila went through such a barren period of twelve years, and yet each day, she returned to her discipline longing for that encounter with the inner light which she knew was still there. Teresa of Calcutta also experienced years of not encountering God in silent prayer but knew the need to continue in her practice.

To be a contemplative is to be dedicated to the practice of daily silent prayer. Whatever distractions, whatever challenges in life, no matter how busy we are, the discipline of contemplation is the work of the Spirit within our souls, and we need to follow this path to become silent and to rest in God.

Exercise One – 'Being Silent'

To be a contemplative, we need to make silence our priority. What marks our spirituality is our practice of praying in silence. This, therefore, is the first principle.

Contemplative prayer is practised by millions of Christians around the world in our day. It is very easy to pray in this way, but it takes a lifetime of practice. The best way to start is to follow the advice of a contemplative, someone who gives the essential teaching.

The following quotation explains how to pray this way. Father John founded the WCCM (www.wccm.org), which holds classes throughout the world:

> Sit down. Sit still and upright. Close your eyes lightly. Sit relaxed but alert. Breathe calmly and regularly. Silently, interiorly begin to say a biblical phrase or a single word. I recommend a prayer-phrase Maranatha, (this is an Aramaic word, the language spoken by Jesus, which means 'come Lord'). Recite it as four syllables of equal length MA-RA-NA-THA. Listen to it as you say it, gently but continuously. Do not think or imagine anything, spiritual or otherwise. If thoughts and images come, these are distractions at the time of meditation, so keep returning to your biblical phrase or word.[181]

Where you pray is up to you. Each contemplative finds their own way. For example, praying in creation is simply a way of

---

[181] Main op. cit. p.8.

using this contemplative style of prayer, often called 'Christian meditation'. Find your own way into that place. It could be a physical location or simply the attitude of your soul in many different places. It can be done in a part of a room in your house set apart with a candle or image to denote the space for yourself and anyone also in your home. It could, though, be your desk at work or in a regular place where you walk. It is possible to hold the space for silence anywhere, inside or outside. The important principle is discipline and the willingness to constantly start over, to become spiritually resilient in longing for your relationship with the divine.

Important principles which will assist you in this practice:
- Decide upon your discipline and stick to it;
- Find your verse or word and use it for a long period, months or years – don't chop and change;
- Find a place in your life where you can commit to holding silence each day, and don't change this unless you have to by external events;
- Decide how long you will keep the silence – ten minutes each day is better than five one day and twenty the next – any length of time up to thirty minutes should be the aim; and,
- Most importantly, don't give up, if it's not working today, begin again tomorrow, the next day and then the next; it is worth persevering.

Chapter Twelve: Being in Community

Benedict advised his followers, 'Find Christ in people'.[182] –
Esther de Waal

The contemplative is never alone. The contemplative is always part of a community. The contemplative is in relationship with Christ. The love of God abides in the contemplative. The contemplative recognises this love in people's hearts, however irritating or annoying they might be. For contemplation is to turn inwards, and in so doing, in finding the inner light, the contemplative is forced to turn outwards to embrace the other in the people around them. As Abba Evagrius advised, the contemplative is 'a person who considers themselves one with all, because one can see themselves in every person'[183]. This is a great truth in contemplation and the second important principle for those seeking to be contemplatives in daily life.

It is ironic that Antony never founded a community. Antony never gave a rule. His way was intensely personal. He retreated into the desert because he could no longer cope with the hypocrisy and double standards of city life. He found in the desert rest in Christ, an inner peace which showed him the way to be obedient to love. Practising hospitality to all strangers and enquirers, he never sought to live with other people. He learnt, though, to come to know Christ in another human heart and to find God in the words and actions of others. Even the first Augustinians who did create a rule and lived in community did

---

[182] De Waal op. cit. p.99.
[183] *Epistula fidei* by Evagrrius Ponticus, written c.379 in Constantinople.

so in a way that is strange to our modern understanding of community. There can be few people who haven't visited an ancient cathedral based on an original Augustinian community and who have looked at what we now call 'choir stalls'. The stalls are for the canons, the word 'canon' meaning in Latin 'list', each with a number and physically separated from one another. This is a reminder that each had their own place, their own number on the list, for them to stand apart from each other to pray in silence. Silent prayer remained the individual activity of Antony and the desert teachers but was held in community. Physically separated but together. For Benedict, though, the community was the context for silent prayer. The members were responsible for and to each other, and the vows of obedience, stability and conversion of life recognised the flow of transformation in the contemplative's life. Being in community was therefore vital to his understanding of contemplation. It is this thread which runs through the contemplative tradition which Franciscans, Carmelites, Jesuits and the modern new monastic communities all share between them.

John Main describes this truth in a memorable comment:

The mutually supporting and suffering dynamic of Christ's mystical body has just this creative aim: the realization of each other's essential being. True community happens in the process of drawing each other into the light of true being. In this process we share a deepening experience of the joy of life, the joy of Being, as we discover more and more of its fullness in a loving faith shared with others. The essence of community then is a recognition of and deep reverence for the Other. Our meditation partakes of this essence because it leads us to turn wholly towards the Other, who is the Spirit in our heart. The full revelation of otherness, and our communion with all is achieved in silence.[184]

I love John Main's phrase that communion is 'the full revelation of otherness'. For him, the other is the divine in our soul; it is the object of our soul's desire, in whom we rest.

For the modern contemplative, we need community as we dedicate our lives to the priority of silence. It is important to know this truth if our practice isn't to become self-serving and selfish. Silent prayer turns us outwards, and in community we experience 'otherness'. For Thomas Merton, this was a sacred unity that all find in contemplation. He comments on the desert fathers and mothers who 'found not only the unification of their own being, not only union with God, but union with one another in the Spirit of God'.[185] The religious communities who followed Benedict's rule also discovered for themselves in humility the unity of otherness. De Waal points to this vital aspect of the rule that 'shows respect for each single person whoever they may be, irrespective of dress, background, professional skill'.[186] The contemplative in community, therefore, is someone who seeks the sacred unity common to each and every soul and in humility seeks to serve those around them in love. The contemplative is therefore called to be Christ-like in community.

This Christ-like contemplative path is a way to understand the example of the great contemplative teachers of the second millennium of Christianity. Francis of Assisi, Teresa of Avila,

---

[184] Main op. cit. p.79.
[185] Merton op. cit. p.17.
[186] De Waal op. cit. p.101.

John of the Cross, Ignatius of Loyola and John Henry Newman all demonstrate for the modern contemplative the way of humility in the love of Christ. Their model of community, which is rooted in personal contemplation, turns them outwards in the service of others, often at great personal cost. The modern contemplative teachers also demonstrate this truth; Dietrich Bonhoeffer's life and fate show that the way of the contemplative is not easy. His clarity of teaching and action in contrast to the established churchmen of his day shows that often to be a contemplative can be a radical and even anarchic path. The contemplative often challenges the status quo and the easy choices to side with the rich and powerful. It is no coincidence that all the new monastic movements who make silent prayer a priority at the same time provide inspirational leadership in challenging social justice. George MacLeod inspired the new Iona community to work across the world amongst the poorest and most disadvantageous. The Taize community is to be found working for reconciliation in the most dangerous parts of the modern world. And who can forget that Brother Roger himself lost his life through his openness to the most needy? Mother Teresa famously inspired her Sisters of Mercy to work with those whom everyone else regarded as untouchable and simply ignored. By showing the love of Christ where it is most needed, the modern contemplative teachers demonstrate that being in community for the sake of otherness is a key principle for anyone who wishes to follow this path in daily life.

Benedict gave his community a new spiritual practice and all of us a new word. Meditation is part of Benedict's practice of Lectio Divina. The 'holy reading' of scripture was of course not new, but Benedict gave his community a unique way of entering into the text to seek to encounter the divine within. Benedict encouraged all to 'soak themselves in scripture'. For Antony, of course, the prime focus of scriptural reading was the gospel, especially the gospel of John. As we hold our silence in community, the practice of reading the Bible, especially the gospels, is as important for us. Often the new monastic communities advise their members to use Lectio Divina as part of the regular pattern of their daily prayers. Personally, I have found the process of reading in this way to be beneficial in approaching many other Christian texts, for example, parts of *The Philokalia*. At the end of this chapter, as a second exercise for those exploring contemplation, I have given a simplified way of using this pattern of Benedictine Lectio. The spiritual practice, though, is now used by many people who are not Benedictine and indeed who do not consider themselves as contemplatives. It is a simple way to enter into the love of Christ.

Being in community is important to a modern contemplative. All contemplative paths offer communal silent prayer as well as encourage daily personal devotion. Like many contemplatives, I find the practice of silent prayer has a slightly different feel when practised in a group as opposed to being done individually. There are many communities to join, and some can be accessed online. As a contemplative in the modern world, we all miss a vital aspect of this life if we always pray alone. Antony came to see this truth, and all who follow in his way need to find a home in the sacred unity of community to know the otherness of Christ's love.

Exercise Two – Lectio Divina

'Lectio Divina' simply means 'holy reading'. It is a traditional Benedictine practice of scriptural reading, meditation and prayer intended to promote communion with God and increase the knowledge of God's Word. Lectio Divina does not treat Scripture as text to be studied but as the Living Word of God.

Lectio differs from the ordinary act of reading and goes beyond the words on the page. The four basic steps are read, meditate, pray and contemplate.

Read

1. The first step is the reading of scripture. In order to achieve a calm and tranquil state of mind, preparation before Lectio Divina is recommended. An example would be sitting quietly and in silence and reciting a prayer inviting the Holy Spirit to guide the reading of the scripture that is to follow.

   When the passage is read, it is generally advised not to try to assign a meaning to it at first but to wait for the action of the Holy Spirit to illuminate the mind, as the passage is pondered upon.

2. The second step in Lectio Divina thus involves meditating upon and pondering on the scriptural passage. To meditate on the passage that has been read, it is held lightly and gently considered from various angles. The emphasis is not on analysis of the passage but on keeping the mind open and allowing the Holy Spirit to inspire a meaning for it.

Benedictine meditation aims to heighten our personal relationship based on the love of God, stimulate thought and deepen our understanding.

3. In the Benedictine tradition, prayer is understood as dialogue with God. It is a loving conversation with God, who has invited us into an embrace.

   Prayer during Lectio Divina can take many forms. It can be praise, petition, thanksgiving – silence can also be a response.

4. Contemplation takes place in terms of silent prayer that expresses love for God.

   Contemplative prayer is 'silence or silent love'. Words in this kind of prayer are not speeches; they are like kindling that feeds the fire of love.

   In this silence, the Father speaks to us his incarnate Word, who suffered, died and rose; in this silence, the Spirit enables us to share in the prayer of Jesus.

Chapter Thirteen: Generous Hospitality

My Rule is to receive you with hospitality and to let you go in peace.[187] *– Antony of Egypt*

The aim of the contemplation is 'quies'. The Latin word 'quies' means 'to rest'. Resting in silence is both the means and the end for the contemplative. The contemplative life is about the priority of silence which helps us turns inwards and then can transforms us turning us outwards. By this means, we come to be in community and appreciate otherness. The transformation then leads the contemplative to live a life of generous hospitality.

Openness to all is a key feature of the life of the desert teachers. Never do they hide from the most difficult questions; their retreat is from the city, which is full of falsehoods, manipulations and hypocrisy. Antony goes into the desert to seek truth and face the harsh reality of himself and the world. He does so in the sure and certain knowledge of Christ's love, which abides in him. Antony's times of being locked in the cemeteries of North Africa strike us as odd. His teaching about evil and the necessity of even the devil having some good within strikes us as radically different teaching. Yet at its heart, Antony's practice and teaching show an openness to God in all things and a willingness to discern God's goodness in relation to the honest truth about the world. For Antony, later in his time in the desert, he came to understand that nothing must get in the way of this generous hospitality. The story of his searching for the holy man leading him to the cobbler's shop at the centre of a town and his conversation remind us of the contemplative need

---

[187] Merton op. cit. p.51.

to hold others in love. The priority was silent prayer for Antony; the discipline that this prayer imposed taught the contemplative all that was required and the necessary turning inwards causing a turning outwards into community, which inevitably leads to the welcome of the alien and the stranger.

This third principle of 'generous hospitality' is well-known to many of the new monastic-style communities and is fundamental to understanding them. This stems from their contemplative life; it is a necessary result of silent prayer and being in community. The Taize community is an example of this generous hospitality; anyone is welcomed to this community on a former French farm. The community itself is made up of one hundred brothers who come from a variety of backgrounds but who are dedicated to sacred unity. Its current rule states:

> By its very existence, the community is a 'parable of community' that wants its life to be a sign of reconciliation between divided Christians and between separated peoples. The brothers of the community live solely by their work. They do not accept donations. Certain brothers live in some of the disadvantaged places in the world, to be witnesses of peace there, alongside people who are suffering. These small groups of brothers in Asia, Africa and South America, share the living conditions of the people around them. They strive to be a presence of love among the very poor, street children, prisoners, the dying, and those who are wounded by broken relationships, or who have been abandoned.[188]

---

[188] www.taize.fr/en_articles6525.html

Taize, of course, as founded by Brother Roger and his friends, began as a contemplative community in 1940 in Vichy France, one of the most dangerous places in the world at that time. Their main reason for being in this part of France was to welcome refugees and those fleeing persecution. Brother Roger placed himself and his companions deliberately in harm's way to have the greatest impact. His contemplative community, like the desert fathers and mothers, stood in direct opposition to the world they lived in for the sake of becoming more Christ-like, resting in God's love.

In a similar way to the Taize community, the worldwide Iona community is committed to generous hospitality. The community is defined as 'an ecumenical movement of men and women from different walks of life and different traditions in the Christian church; committed to the gospel of Jesus Christ, and to follow where that leads, even into the unknown; engaged together, and with people of good will across the world, in acting, reflecting and praying for justice, peace and integrity of creation; and, convinced that the inclusive community we seek must be embodied in the community we practice'.[189] Inspired by the example of Bonhoeffer and resulting from his own conversion experience in the trenches of the First World War, George MacLeod envisioned a new Iona community. As the community's vision demonstrates, it is 'inclusive', seeking to practice a generous hospitality in its openness to everyone. This is rooted in Celtic spirituality with the example of Columba (Columcille) as the founder of the original Iona community; a community which had its inspiration from the contemplative model of Ninian and Patrick influenced by the desert teachers.

---

[189] https://iona.org.uk

Iona itself inspired others, notably the Corrymeela community, which was founded on similar principles and which, like Taize, sought to bring reconciliation to one of the most dangerous places in the world. At the heart of 'The Troubles' in Ireland, when sectarian murders were an everyday occurrence and a person could be killed by a malicious word for being a suspected informant or sympathiser for the 'wrong side', this courageous community was created by Protestants and Roman Catholics. Founded in 1965 by Ray Davey and students from Queens University Belfast, the community grew out of a simple vision:

> promoting tolerance between people of different backgrounds and beliefs, Corrymeela offers space for an analysis of the underlying dynamics of conflict, fracture, scapegoating and violence that we see across so many spheres of our world today.[190]

The generous hospitality of the contemplative tradition is found in many different forms, one of the most striking for its rapid development over the last twenty years is the 'Local House of Prayer' movement (LHOP). Inspired by Roy and Daphne Goodwin at Ffald y Brenin, this movement is now worldwide. Roy's best-selling books *The Grace Outpouring* and *Blessing Course* have been copied in many parts of the world. The local house of prayer can be started with just two or three people and offers 'a framework to help us align our lives for greater blessing and to impact our world for Jesus Christ where we are'.[191] The dynamic of the LHOP movement is to hold those

---

[190] www.corrymeela.org/about

[191] www.localhouseofprayer.org

within the immediate area in prayer; often this is a contemplative group who have their own 'rule of life' and are committed to prayer. Holding their lives and place in silent prayer. Exercise Three at the end of this chapter offers an experience of 'holding in love' those among whom we live, offering silent prayer as a means of generous hospitality rooted in a contemplative experience.

Perhaps the best known contemplative community in our own day is the WCCM, which places silent prayer at its heart. All that it stands for follows this contemplative practice, and generous hospitality flows out from the silence. The WCCM describes its role and purpose in the following fivefold vision of Christian meditation:

> Firstly, the faith with which you meditate, some sense of personal connection with Jesus. Secondly, the historical and theological tradition in which we meditate. Thirdly the sense of community it leads to: "when two or three pray together in my name, I am there among them". Fourthly, the other means by which our spiritual life is nourished; like scripture, sacraments and worship. Finally, we meditate in order to take the attention off ourselves. In the Christian tradition, contemplation is seen as a grace and a reciprocal work of love. Not surprisingly then if we find we become more loving people as a result of meditating, this will express itself in all of our relationships, our work and our sense of service especially to those in any kind of need.[192]

---

[192] www.wccm.org/content/what-meditation

Soul Desire   151

Generous hospitality is therefore the outpouring of Antony's own teaching that in all things we should be obedient to love. For those of us seeking to be contemplative in daily life, we cannot ignore this third principle. Flowing out from silent prayer and being in community constitute the call to generous hospitality in our lives.

Exercise Three – 'Holding in Loving Prayer'

This contemplative exercise is not the same as intercessory prayer. In this holding prayer exercise, we do not ask for anything. Rather, as in the stories of Aidan of Lindisfarne, we simply hold in our loving hearts those around us and seek to discern God's peace.

The practice of 'holding prayer":

1. Begin in silent prayer. Whatever your practice, use this at the beginning;
2. Use your imagination to 'walk out' from where you are praying. Walk down the street and pray for each place you pass. Pray for those who live there, for those who work and for any other activity taking place. Do not go too far in your prayer, but keep to the place you live and those who are your near neighbours;
3. Having held those closest to you in prayer, enter into a second time of silent prayer, but in your soul, bring those whom you have prayed for with you;
4. Finally, use the following or similar holding prayer to bring this time to a close:

> Loving Jesus,
> give peace to my soul,
> give peace to my home,
> give peace to my neighbours,
> give peace to my street,
> give peace to the community where I live,
> that each place may know your love,
> that each street may know your love,
> that each heart may know your love,

that each home may know your love,
that my soul may know your love,
this moment, this hour, this day and for evermore.
Amen.

This is a simple prayer practice which can be added to any other time of prayer. You might find it helpful to have a simple street plan to remind you of the places and people to hold in prayer. Of course, you can always pray in this way for other places and people. The key is to add this to your time of contemplation and keep your practice as simple as possible. This prayer isn't about advocating any course of action but rather holding in love those who are in your soul's silent prayer.

Chapter Fourteen: Attentive Living

In order to keep our balance, we need to hold the interior and exterior, visible and invisible, known and unknown, temporal and eternal, ancient and new, together.[193] *– John O'Donohue*

To be a contemplative is to be attentive. Attentive to yourself, your mind, your heart and your soul. The discipline required to maintain the priority of silent prayer is about being attentive. There is the need to be attentive in the practice of daily silence. You must become attentive to your prayer word, your verse, your scripture or recitation of the Jesus prayer. This practice of musing becomes part of who you are and how you live. Eventually, it does not require effort, thought or will; it simply comes to you the moment when you turn to prayer. If you have been practising silent prayer faithfully and regularly over a long period, you might even have the experience when you are ill or tired that you hear your inner voice saying your prayer word without any conscious effort. The contemplative is attentive to that inner space, a place where you can return over and over again, your own 'thin place' within your soul. This is the place where, in Celtic spirituality, heaven and earth come closest and where we feel most at home. We need to learn the discipline of being attentive in our contemplation, which has the power to change and transform us. The desert teachers said that your cell would teach you all you needed to know, and I believe that this is what they meant; the daily discipline of attentive living is the great teacher of our souls.

---

[193] *Anam Cara* by John O'Donohue, Bantam Books, 1999 p.14.

Attentive living is therefore the fourth principle on which the contemplative life is based. The modern contemplative needs to make silence their priority. We need to find the space and time to be silent. We need, through this silence, to also recognise that we are part of a community of contemplatives; for us, this might not be a physical group or a geographical location. Being in community, though, is as important to us as it was to Antony or any other religious over the past seventeen centuries. Silence and community then lead us to openness and acceptance of otherness – generous hospitality. In doing all this, we need to live attentively. Being a contemplative isn't about being passive; it is rather being active. Our discipline of silence requires us to be decisive and to know what it is we are looking for, and in turn, this requires us to live in the moment. As Antony told those who came to him on many occasions, it is what happens now in this moment which is important, not yesterday or tomorrow. Of course, being attentive to the present moment is exactly what Jesus taught his disciples, which is recorded for us in the gospels. If we listen and soak ourselves in the words of scripture, we will become aware that our attention is to be focused on the here and now.

Thomas Keating, in writing about centring prayer, encourages us to be caught in the intimate immediacy of the divine within: 'We rarely think of the air we breathe, yet it is in us and around us all the time. In similar fashion, the presence of God penetrates us, is all around us, is always embracing us'.[194] If we are attentive to our bodies, we can feel ourselves breathing in and out, we can relax our heart rate and become still. In the same way in our souls, as we become attentive to our prayer word or verse, we can drive out the distractions of our mind and

---

[194] Keating op. cit. p.21.

Soul Desire

all thoughts and become peaceful and at rest as we become aware of the presence of God around us and within us. John O'Donohue says of each person:

> You are the one and only threshold of inner world. Wholesome-ness is holiness. To be holy is to be natural; to befriend the worlds that come to balance in you. Behind the façade of image and distraction, each person is an artist in this primal and inescapable sense. Each one of us is privileged to be an inner artist who carries and shapes a unique world.[195]

O'Donohue uses the lyrical language of a poet to express this inner beauty but reminds us that it is through our attention to this inner world that we enter, just as he says we are the threshold. Martin Laird, in a similar way, says we are the doorway, and both writers remind us that Jesus says to us in John's gospel that he is the door of our spiritual lives. The vocation of the contemplative life is known in attentive living.

Antony repeatedly encouraged his enquirers to look beyond their studies and books to be attentive to the world around them. It is from him that we have received the origin of the saying of the two books of revelation from God: the first being the scriptures in their broadest sense or at the very least the Protestant Bible, and the second being the whole of creation. J Philip Newell picks up this sense of the contemplative being attentive in creation in his book *Listening for the Heartbeat of God,* where he writes:

---

[195] Anam Cara op. cit. p.15.

God has not created everything out of nothing, but out of his own essence, out of his very life. This is the light that is in all things, the light which is the light of the angels, the light of the created universe, the light indeed of all visible and invisible existence. The world is therefore a visible manifestation of God.[196]

O'Donohue also picks up this sense of God being at work in all creation and his vitality being the ground of our being. His sense is very much that of God being one with us in the revelation of creation. If we are attentive to his presence, we are never alone; O'Donohue sees this truth in commenting of the importance of starting something new and different in our lives:

> Beginnings often frighten us because they seem like lonely voyages into the unknown. Yet in truth no beginning is empty or isolated. Shelter and energy come alive when a beginning is embraced. A beginning is ultimately an invitation to open towards the gifts and growth that are stored up for us.[197]

To be a contemplative is to be aware of God. To be attentive to the divine within but also without. The tradition of Caim prayer in Celtic spirituality evokes this great truth. Significantly, the spiritual practice is best undertaken outside, in the creation which is all around us. Caim is a Gaelic word that means 'protection' and is more commonly referred to as 'circling prayer'. Its most well-known form is from St Patrick's breastplate, dating from sometime in the fifth century:

---

[196] Newell op. cit. p.35.
[197] *Blessings* op. cit. p.20.

Christ with me,
Christ before me, Christ behind me,
Christ in me,
Christ beneath me, Christ above me,
Christ on my right, Christ on my left,
Christ when I lie down,
Christ when I sit down,
Christ when I arise,
Christ in the heart of everyone who thinks of me,
Christ in the mouth of everyone who speaks of me,
Christ in every eye that sees me,
Christ in every ear that hears me.

Caim prayer uses the imagination to know God all around us and to recognise his hand in everything we see and touch. Through this attentiveness, we can come to live in the moment and know that all life is lived in God's goodness.

Knowing God in creation is as much as a learnt skill as practising our prayer word to keep our primary silence. In the same way, as we know how to come daily to that silence to enter the inner life, just as surely to be able to live 'attentively', we need to know how to do this and to practise this regularly. In 2013, when I was researching my book *Walking into Celtic Spirituality,* holding pilgrimages to places associated with the Celtic saints of the first millennium, I sought to undertake silent prayer in creation. As I practised this every day, I became aware of two impulses: first, to seek out water – a stream, river, lake or the sea – and second, to walk. In the seven years that have followed, it hasn't always been possible to achieve the former, but the second is my daily practice. I see this as a key part of my life as a contemplative. Daily silent prayer in attentive walking is part of my contemplative practice. The important part of this spiritual walking as a contemplative is always to try to remain in the moment. It is the attention to the immediate presence and reality of the life in creation all around and within which is the purpose of this contemplative prayer walking. It is important not to allow thoughts to drift in and out, thinking about the past or what is happening next. Often something will arrest my immediate attention which otherwise I would have missed. Sometimes this will be something of nature: a flower, animal or a landscape, the rain or a sun beam. However, often it will be something entirely unexpected: the logo on a van, the shape of a building or the conversation of someone passing. At the end of this chapter, the fourth spiritual exercise I recommend is 'attentive prayer walking'; this is very simple to start and do, and it can be done in many ways and will add to the practice of contemplation. It is a skill, the attention of 'being in the moment'.

All this is about being in the moment, being aware, being fully alive. The charismatic Anglican bishop John V Taylor caught this spiritual sense of attentive living in his brief book *A Matter of Life and Death* when he wrote:

> It has long been my conviction that God is not hugely concerned as to whether we are religious or not. What matters to God, and matters supremely, is whether we are alive or not. If your religion brings you more fully to life, God will be in it; but if your religion inhibits your capacity for life or makes you run away from it, you may be sure God is against it.[198]

---

[198] *A Matter of Life and Death* by John V Taylor, SCM, London, 1986, p.18.

Attentive living is about being alive. The word, usually translated from Hebrew as 'spirit', 'breathe' or 'wind' in the Old Testament, is 'rauch'. It is the rauch that moves over the face of the water at the moment of creation in the book of Genesis, and it is rauch that Ezekiel is told to prophesy over the dry bones. Rauch is simply 'aliveness', and as contemplatives, we are seeking to become fully alive, as Jesus promises in John's gospel, to live the full life. As well as daily attentive prayer, walking my life as a contemplative is marked by longer pilgrimage walking. Long walks are good for us not just spiritually but also mentally and physically. Shane O'Mara, a consultant neurologist, writes of the benefits of walking:

> The core lesson is this: walking enhances every aspect of our social, psychological and neural functioning. It is simple, life-enhancing, health-building prescription we all need, one that we should take in regular doses, large and small, at a good pace, day in, day out, in nature and in our towns and cities. We need to make walking a natural habitual part of everyday lives.[199]

Walking at our own pace attentive to the immediate space around us for several days gives the contemplative a sense of the immediate presence of God and connects us with the divine in creation. It makes us feel truly alive and helps us recognise the aliveness of the divine and God around us.

---

[199] *In Praise of Walking* by Shane O'Mara, Bodley Head, London, 2019, p.182.

Exercise Four – Attentive Walking

This practice is from Celtic spirituality. For those who are not physically able to walk, it can be done as an imaginative spiritual exercise. The walk doesn't have to be long or demanding; it is rather the experience of being totally attentive to each moment that is crucial. The process is simple:

1. Set aside a time and space for your attentive walk.
2. Ensure you have everything that you need, e.g., the correct footwear and outer clothing; bad weather is not an excuse. A walk in heavy rain or a gale can be invigorating.
3. Walk at your own pace. Each of us has a speed which is comfortable for ourselves. Find your own pace.
4. Walk quietly without any distractions. Turn your phone off, and try to walk without interruption.
5. As you begin to walk, turn on all your senses: look with your eyes, hear with your ears, smell with your nose, taste with your mouth and feel the ground beneath your feet with your steady footsteps.
6. Don't allow yourself to be distracted by anything you were doing before the walk or anything you will need to do after; live in the moment.
7. Expect to be surprised. Allow your senses to notice and stop to experience the moment as it is revealed to you.

This practice, if repeated regularly, will begin to teach you about your own spiritual journey and will gently unfold for you your true contemplative nature.

Chapter Fifteen: Loving Reconciliation

Waiting all upon God in that which is of God, you are kept open to receive the teachings of God. And the pure wisdom and knowledge is that which is to know God and Jesus Christ, the way and to walk out of your own ways and out of your own thoughts.[200] – George Fox

To be a contemplative is to attempt to be reconciled to yourself. George Fox understood the need to discover the inner light which enlightens every human soul. Antony and the ancient desert teachers talk about this as resting in God. For modern contemplatives, we need also to come to this fifth principle in living the contemplative way in daily life. George Fox and modern Quakers speak of walking, cheerfully recognising God in each person. To do this, though, we need to walk with a spirit of thankfulness and gratitude for all that we have received. We need to recognise the importance of the loving heart, which was so important to the desert fathers and mothers.

As someone who has been a spiritual director for over thirty-five years, I recognise that all 'spiritual problems' can be summed up in one sentence. Most people find it is impossible to believe that God loves them just as they are; we find 'unconditional love' almost impossible to accept. What is the message of Jesus to us in John's gospel? The Word made flesh is the love of God. God's love which is so great that he lays down his life for us. It is the love that abides in us as we abide in him. It is the love that we are commanded to show in all we say, do, think or feel. It is

---

[200] *The Works of George Fox* by George Fox, New York, 1831, p.28.

this love by which the world will know that we are the disciples of Jesus. It is in this love that God overcomes the world. It is in this love that Mary Magdalene, Peter and John, together with the rest of the disciples, are restored at Easter. The whole gospel is about the power of unconditional love and that this love is God's nature, character and purpose – so why do we find it so difficult to accept? This book is too short to answer this question; it is simply important for us to note that it is a problem for us as contemplatives as well.

The unanswerable question is also at the heart of understanding Antony's motives in retreating to the desert. In this book, I have repeated the understanding handed down by tradition that he sought to escape the hypocrisy and corruption of his times, and of course, on one level, this must be true. However, his extreme behaviour in being locked in the graves and wrestling his own demons speaks to the modern psychological knowledge of the need to be reconciled to himself. Often his traumatic experiences are overlooked because they are only alluded to by the first writers. We have no biography of Antony, and we know of one sister but little else. Whom had Antony lost to the persecution of Christianity by the imperial cult? How could he accept the unconditional love of God when so many he had loved had been betrayed and died in the arena, mauled to death by wild animals? In modern terms, did he suffer from 'survivor guilt'? Is this also what drives him to be 'holy', and why does it worry him so much that he seeks out one holier than himself? There are many questions about Antony, but it is reassuring for us who seek the contemplative life that he appears to have found that accepting he was loved unconditionally was as hard for him as it is for us.

Other contemplatives know the struggle to accept God's love all too well. Brother Roger writes:

Could the call to reconciliation ever invite passivity or life without struggle? No, the gospel has never led to tranquility. Being reconciled with oneself, as with others, supposes a readiness to accept tension and struggles. By neutralizing or fleeing situations of crisis, vital energy is destroyed. Passing through crises, looking beyond is a road that takes us far.[201]

The acceptance of unconditional love is therefore a lifetime journey which includes many times of darkness and struggle. The extreme experience of John of the Cross when he was kidnapped and tortured to renounce his faith is perhaps an example of a contemplative faith that grows to find love in struggle. John was punished by imprisonment in 1577. A cell was made for him in the monastery that was so small he could barely lie on the floor and couldn't stand upright. He was fed only bread and water and occasional scraps of salt fish. Each week, he was taken into a public place and lashed and then returned to his cell. Yet this contemplative, who had suffered so much later, wrote, 'Wisdom enters through love, silence, and mortification. It is great wisdom to know how to be silent and to look at neither the remarks, nor the deeds, nor the lives of others'.[202] John came to know the unconditional love of God, which alone could transform his suffering and bring him to accept the divine in darkness; this a remarkable level of assurance that few achieve but which the desert teachers sought to find rest in God. John concludes that 'in the evening of life, we will be judged on love alone'.[203]

---

[201] Brico op. cit. p.172.
[202] *The Dark Night of the Soul* by St John of the Cross, Dover Publications, New York p.61
[203] Ibid, p.72

This fifth and final principle of living as a contemplative is challenging for us all. To seek loving reconciliation is part of the contemplative life to achieve our rest in God. John Main perceived that this gift of unconditional love needed to be fully realised in reconciliation. Reconciliation with ourselves in our inner life, though, cannot be separated from reconciliation without ourselves, with those around us, with those we dislike, with our enemies, with those we would rather ignore or simply wish would go away. For our reconciliation, we need other people. Main writes of this great truth:

What love means is rejoicing in the otherness of the other because the depth of this awareness is the depth of our communion with the other. In this communion the discovery of our own true self and that of the other is the same discovery. So in the people we live with we find not objects to be cast in our own superficial likeness but, much more, we find in them our true selves, for our true selves only appear, only become realised, when we are wholly turned toward another.[204]

As a result, it should be no surprise to us that all the modern contemplative communities throughout the world see themselves engaged in the work of reconciliation. For reconciliation is essential to us in contemplation if we are to see ourselves as God sees us. We can only come to the knowledge of unconditional love if we accept with a thankful heart this encounter with Jesus, who shows to us the love of the Father, which indwells our souls but helps us recognise this same truth in the lives of those around us.

---

[204] Main op. cit. p.78.

Part of the revival in the contemporary world of contemplation has been driven by the increasing use of Ignatian spirituality exercises. Exercise Five, which concludes this chapter and this book, is one of the most popular. Many people use the prayer of 'The Examen' daily. They are not Jesuits and indeed not religious. Indeed, some may be seekers of faith rather than confessing Christians, but the simplicity of Ignatian spirituality and the use of imagination are strongly attractive to many people. In this fifth principle of living a contemplative life, the practice of 'colloquy' advocated by Ignatius can open for us a way into the loving heart of Jesus. By imagining him in our daily lives and seeking to talk through with him our day, we can gain an insight into practically what unconditional love might mean and look like. The practice in 'The Examen' of meditation upon one event or conversation for which we are thankful can transform our attitude towards our life over a period of time. Many people keep a spiritual journal and record each day the one thing that they are led to give thanks for in 'The Examen' prayer. In so doing, over the days, weeks, months and years that this record grows and grows, they can begin to see the power of God's unconditional love to change and transform every life.

Conclusion – Being a contemplative in daily life

In the last chapters of this book, I have presented what I believe to be the final principles on which anyone can live a contemplative life. The five principles are as follows:

- The priority of silence,
- Being in community,
- Practising generous hospitality,
- Attentive living, and
- Seeking loving reconciliation.

We don't need to be a full-time professional Christian; wherever we are, whatever we do, however we live these principles can help us keep on track and follow the example of Antony, the ancient desert teachers and the advice of the contemporary contemplative teachers to find our own way to rest in God. These principles are, though, in one sense arbitrary and subjective. They appear to me to be most helpful and to have been advocated by many contemplative writers. George Fox, though, is correct in his advice that for us the only path is to walk out of our ways and come to know God's ways. At the beginning of the introduction, I told the story of Antony's own teaching that our own soul's desire can teach us how to find God in our lives. The contemplative path is part of God's call, and in walking in this way, we must be true to our own soul, and in doing this, we will come to rest in God and to come to know his unconditional love for each and every soul.

Exercise Five – The Examen

Jim Manney's book on the prayer of 'The Examen' is very accessible, and he describes it as follows:

The Examen is a method of reviewing your prayer in the presence of God. Here it is in a nutshell:

1. Ask God for light. I want to look at my day with God's eyes, not merely my own
2. Give thanks. Be grateful
3. Review the day. I carefully look back on the day just completed being guided by the Holy Spirit.
4. Face your shortcomings. I face up to what is wrong, in my life and me.
5. Look toward the day to come. I ask where I need God in the day to come[205]

The way of praying first used by Ignatius and his followers resonates in the modern mind. His almost conversational style is so helpful to those put off by the formality of Christian worship. The concentration on the person of Jesus is refreshingly simple amid all the 'doctrines' of the church. Jim Manney sums it up as follows:

The Examen isn't the only way to pray but it's a way that everyone can pray. It banishes the abstract and relishes the concrete. It is inexhaustible. It treats every moment of everyday as a blessed time when God can appear. It's a way to find God in all things.[206]

---

[205] Jim Manney, *A Simple Life-changing Prayer*, Loyola Press, Chicago, 2011, p.1.
[206] Ibid., p.4.

Postscript

This book is written for those who are seeking the contemplative life. It is necessarily a brief overview of the deep spirituality which is represented by nearly twenty centuries of Christian contemplation. As such the book barely scratches the surface of Christian apophatic spirituality.

The purpose of the book is to encourage. To encourage those who are not religious professionals. To encourage those who seek the contemplative way amid busy modern living. At the beginning of the introduction I included a quotation from Antony. He advised, 'whatever you see your soul desire according to God, do that thing and you shall keep your heart safe'. [207] This is the best advice for anyone beginning to explore the contemplative path.

If we are to value silence and meditation we need to trust in the contemplative relationship and allow ourselves to experience the love of God. This experience will teach us everything we need to know. God's love taught Anthony and in the same way this love alone can transform our lives.

---

[207] *The Wisdom of the Desert*, Thomas Merton, New Directions, New York, 1960, p.25.

Further Reading

The Edge of Glory by David **Adam**, Triangle, 1985

Encompassing God by David **Adam**, SPCK, 2014

*Life of St Anthony of Egypt by St **Athanasius** of Alexandra*, translated by Philip Schaff and Henry Wace, Pantianos Classics, first published 1892.

Experiencing God in a time of crisis by Sarah **Bachelard**, Meditatio, London, 2017

Prayer and Righteous Action by Eberhard **Bethage**, SCM, 1980

The Cost of Discipleship by Dietrich **Bonheoffer**, SCM, 1964

Letters and Papers from Prison by Dietrich **Bonheoffer**, Macmillan, 1972

Centering Prayer and Inner Awakening by Cynthia **Bourgeault,** Cowley, 2004

Colonies of Heaven by Ian **Bradley**, DLT, London, 2000

Taize by Rex **Brico**, Collins, London, 1978

The New Monasticism: A Manifesto for Contemplative Living by Adam **Bucko** and Rory McEntee, Orbis, 2015

*John **Cassian** Conferences,* Paulist Press, 1985

The Age of the Saints in the Early Celtic Church by Nora **Chadwick**, OUP, 1961

Seeking God: The Way of St Benedict, by Esther **de Waal** (many editions first published 1984)

The desert mothers by Mary **Earle**, Morehouse, 2007

On Living Simply Homilies of **St John Chrysostom**, Liguori Publications, 1997

To Live as Francis Lived, the Path of Franciscan Spirituality by Leonard **Fole**, Jovian Weigel and Patti Normile, St Anthony Messenger Press, 2000

The Works of George Fox by George **Fox**, New York, 1831

Light Within by Laurence **Freeman**, OSB, Canterbury Press, Norwich, 1986

Melodies of New Monasticism: Boneoffer's Vision and Iona's Witness by Craig **Gardner**, SCM, 2018

Christian Meditation by Paul **Harris**, DLT, London, 1996

To be a Pilgrim by Basil **Hume**, SPCK, 1986

The Dark Night of the Soul by **St John of the Cross**, Dover Publications, London, 2003

Memory and Identity by **John Paul II**, Weidenfeld & Nicolson, London, 2005

Into the Silent Land by Martin **Laird**, DLT, 2006

Sunlit Absence by Martin **Laird**, OUP, New York, 2011

Intimacy with God by Thomas **Keating**, Crossroads, 2009

Word into Silence: A Manual for Christian Meditation by John **Main**, Canterbury, 2006

A simple life changing prayer by Jim **Manney**, Loyola, 2011

Total Cost and Total Transformation by Helen **Marshall**, Grove Books, 2011

The Impact of God by Iain **Matthew**, Hodder & Stoughton, 1995

The Wisdom of the Desert, Thomas **Merton**, New Directions, New York, 1960

Bonheoffer by Eric **Metaxes,** Nelson, 2011

A New Monastic Handbook: From Vision to Practice by Ian **Mobsby**, Canterbury Press, 2013

Listening for the Heartbeat of God by J Philip **Newell**, SPCK, London, 2008

Anam Cara by John **O'Donohue**, Bantam Books, 1999

Benedictus by John **O'Donohue** , Bantam Press, London, 2007

In Praise of Walking by Shane **O'Mara**, Bodley Head, London, 2019

The soul of a pilgrim by Christine **Paintner**, Ave Marie Press, 2015

The Artist Rule: Nuturing your creative heart, by Christine **Paintner**, Ave Marie Press, 2011

*The Confession of **Saint Patrick*** translated by John Skinner, Doubleday, New York, 1998

*Early Fathers from the **Philokalia*** translated by E Kadloubovsky and G E H Palmer, Faber and Faber, London, 1954

*Writings from the **Philokalia** on Prayer of the Heart* translated by E Kadloubovsky and G E H Palmer, Faber and Faber, London, 1951

*The **Philokalia** Volume 1* translated by G E H Palmer, Philip Sherrard, and Kallistos Ware, Faber and Faber, London, 1979

Franciscan Spirituality: Following St Francis Today by Brother **Ramon** SSF, SPCK, 2008

Heaven on Earth by Brother **Ramon**, Marshall Pickering, London 1991

The Divine Dance by Richard **Rohr**, SPCK, London, 2016

Immortal Diamond: The Search for Our True Self by Richard **Rohr**, SPCK, 2013

Just This: Prompts and Practices for Contemplation by Richard **Rohr**, SPCK, 2018

Falling Upwards by Richard **Rohr**, SPCK, London, 2012

Silence: A User's Guide by Maggie **Ross**, DLT, 2014

Landmarks: an Ignatian Journey by Margaret **Silf**, DLT, 1998

Exploring Celtic Spirituality by Ray **Simpson**, Kevin Mayhew, Suffolk, 2004

Turned by Divine Love by John **Stroyan**, BRF, London, 2019

St Francis of Assisi by Jon **Sweeney**, Griffin, 2019

A Matter of Life and Death by John V **Taylor**, SCM, London, 1986

Interior Castle by **Teresa of Avila**, translated by E Allison Peters, Dover Publications, New York, 2007

Chiara Lubich: A Biography by Armando **Torno**, New City Press, New York 2012

The Cloud of Unknowing edited by Evelyn **Underhill**, St Anthanasius Press, 2017

Mysticism by Evelyn **Underhill**, Aziloth Books, 2011
The Carmelite Way by John **Welch**, Gracewing, 1996
Silence and Honey Cakes by Rowan **Williams**, Lion, 2004
The Kentigern Way by Stephen **Wright**, Wild Goose Publications, Iona, 2019

Index

About the author

Cameron Butland lives in Cumbria. He is a member of the Cumbria Ecumenical Spirituality Group, (CESG). CESG trains spiritual directors and manages the Christian spiritual directors' network for Cumbria. He regularly leads quiet days and courses. His other books include: Work in Worship; Our Daily Bread; Walking into Celtic Spirituality; and Growing Spirituality.